Cars

Robert Wyatt

Macdonald Educational

Managing Editor Chris Milsome
Editor Anne Furniss
Illustrators John Stewart
 Brian Hiley
 William Hobson
 Robert Corrall
 Tony Mitchell
 Jack Pelling
Illustrations consultant John W. Wood
Projects R. H. Warring
Picture Research Marion Gain, Ann Usborne,
 Penny Warn, Mary Walsh

First published 1971
Reprinted 1972 (twice), 1973
Second edition 1974
Reprinted 1977
Macdonald Educational
Holywell House
Worship Street
London EC2A 2EN

contents

Ancestors of the car	3
The petrol engine; four-stroke cycle	4
The race for speed, 1894-1905	6
Secrets of the car; important parts	8
Motoring for gentlemen; car sales until 1914	10
The first popular car; the Model 'T' Ford	12
The motoring craze in the 1920's	14
Cars and people	16
Racing in the 20's and 30's	18
Mass production; the assembly line	20
The family car	22
The 'Beetle'; the incredible Volkswagen	24
The Big Car Countries	26
General Motors; the world's giant	28
The sports car	30
Launching a new car	32
Record breaking	34
Blessing or disaster; problems of the car era	36
Grand Prix racing	38
The death toll and the safety revolution	40
Wankels' new engine	41
Experimental cars for the future	42
Projects supplement; streamlining	43
Projects; How to be a car designer	44
Projects; Building and improving a car design	46
Index	47-48
Metric conversion table	48

ISBN 0356 03692 8

Printed and bound by
New Interlitho, Milan, Italy

Ancestors of the car

The wheel is born

Thousands of years ago people lived in small groups in caves and huts and did not need to travel very far. When they did travel, they walked, or rode on horseback.

As the population grew, people began to sell things to other groups. They carried their goods on pack horses, and as they walked and rode they made tracks across the country and through the forests.

Trading increased and people wanted to carry more things over longer distances. So they began to use wheeled carts. No one knows who first thought of the wheel, but it was used a long time ago in China and Egypt. The wheeled carts made the tracks wider until they became roads.

Steam engines

Wheeled carts were very slow, and rich people drove in fast chariots and carriages. Stage coaches ran between all the big cities. These horse-drawn vehicles were quite fast and could go ten miles in an hour (10mph).

The railway steam engine was introduced in about 1830. Trains were quick and comfortable, but they needed rails. Steam road vehicles could go anywhere there was a road, but they were heavy and slow. Someone had to make an engine that could do the work of a horse. It took a long time to find the right answer.

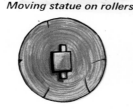

Moving statue on rollers

Before the wheel was invented, heavy things were pushed along on rollers. These Egyptians used wooden rollers to move large heavy objects.

Early solid and spoked wheels

The first wheels were solid wooden discs. They were so heavy that the carts could not go very fast. Wheels with spokes used less wood, so they were lighter. The spoked wheel is also very strong.

The Romans fixed their chariots on to two wheels which were held in position on a wooden axle. The driver had to stand up or he would have been thrown out every time the chariot went over a bump.

Roman chariot

An early French suspended carriage

A carriage used in France 200 years ago (left) is in two parts. The wheels are still on axles, but are fitted to a separate part called a chassis. The body is suspended from the chassis by leather straps, so that passengers do not feel the bumps.

This is one of the steam carriages used over 100 years ago. Two men were needed to work it: a driver to steer at the front and a stoker at the back to put coal into the boiler. It looked like a horse-drawn carriage and was heavy and slow.

James' steam carriage 1829

In Great Britain in 1865, no steam vehicles were allowed to go faster than 4mph in the country or 2mph in towns. Until 1878, by law, a man had to walk in front with a red flag.

The petrol engine four-stroke cycle

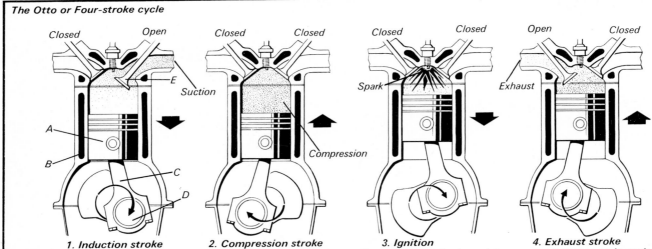

The Otto or Four-stroke cycle

| Closed | Open | Closed | Closed | Closed | Closed | Open | Closed |

E / Suction / A / B / C / D — Spark / Compression — Exhaust

1. Induction stroke
The Otto, or four-stroke cycle: A round metal piston (A) moves up and down in an iron cylinder (B). A metal connecting rod (C) connects the piston to the crank (D). The crank turns a heavy flywheel, and keeps the piston moving.

In the first stroke—the suc-

2. Compression stroke
tion stroke—the righthand valve (E) is open. The piston, which fits tightly in the cylinder, comes down and air and petrol vapour is sucked into the cylinder. It is like sucking air into a bicycle pump by drawing back the handle.

When the cylinder is full the

3. Ignition
valve shuts and the piston moves up for the compression stroke. The gas is squashed into a small space, or compressed, because it cannot get out. In this state it is highly explosive. When the piston gets to the top a spark lights the gas and it explodes. The expanded gas

4. Exhaust stroke
cannot escape so it pushes the piston down the cylinder to give the power stroke. Then the piston exhausts the waste gas. In the first engines this happened about 50 times every minute. A modern engine can turn round thousands of times a minute.

Gas engines were sometimes used to drive machinery. A piston moved up and down in the cylinder and a crank changed this action into a circular motion. These engines did not compress the gas, so were slow and low-powered. However, in the 1870s, a German named Otto worked out a four-stroke cycle. Now the piston made four separate movements, or strokes, with different jobs being done with each stroke. The same idea is used in the petrol engines of nearly all cars today.

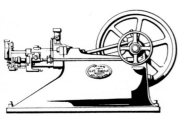

Gas engine using Otto Cycle 1880

Daimler engine 1883

The gas engine

By 1860 Lenoir, a Belgian, was making and selling engines that ran on gas. In 1863 he fitted one in a car which he drove for six miles around Paris. The journey took between two and three hours, because his engine was very slow. It could only turn a hundred times in a minute. Marcus, an Austrian built a crude four wheeler in 1864; his 1874 car could travel at 5mph.

The petrol engine

Like the wheel, the petrol engine was not invented by one man. Many engineers and inventors were working on the idea. Daimler was a German engineer. He built Otto engines and designed a successful petrol engine with one cylinder in 1883. It ran at 900 revolutions per minute (rpm). In 1885, Daimler built an experimental motor cycle and a four-wheeled car. Daimler's idea was to convert horse carriages into horseless carriages by fitting an engine under the carriage. The shafts could be replaced by a steering gear to steer the front wheels.

Daimler

Daimler produced the first high-speed petrol engine in the world, and many other makers used it. Emile Levassor, in France, was one. In 1891, his firm began building *Panhard et Levassor* cars which makers all over the world imitated for the next ten years.

Benz, the son of a German engine-driver, was an exception. He invented his own engine and made the first petrol cars designed for sale. The first car he made, in 1885, had three wheels. The engine was slower than Daimler's. It would only go very slowly along a flat road. Cars he made in the next two years were much better. One of them, made in 1887, had a top speed of 12mph.

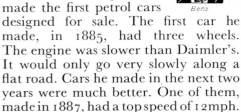

Benz

First cars for sale

A Frenchman, Roger, first marketed Benz cars in 1888. It was some time before the cars could be used on the roads without frightening horses or being chased by policemen! A Benz car was brought to England and is now in the Science Museum in London. It cost £130, which was a lot of money when a skilled workman earned £1 a week.

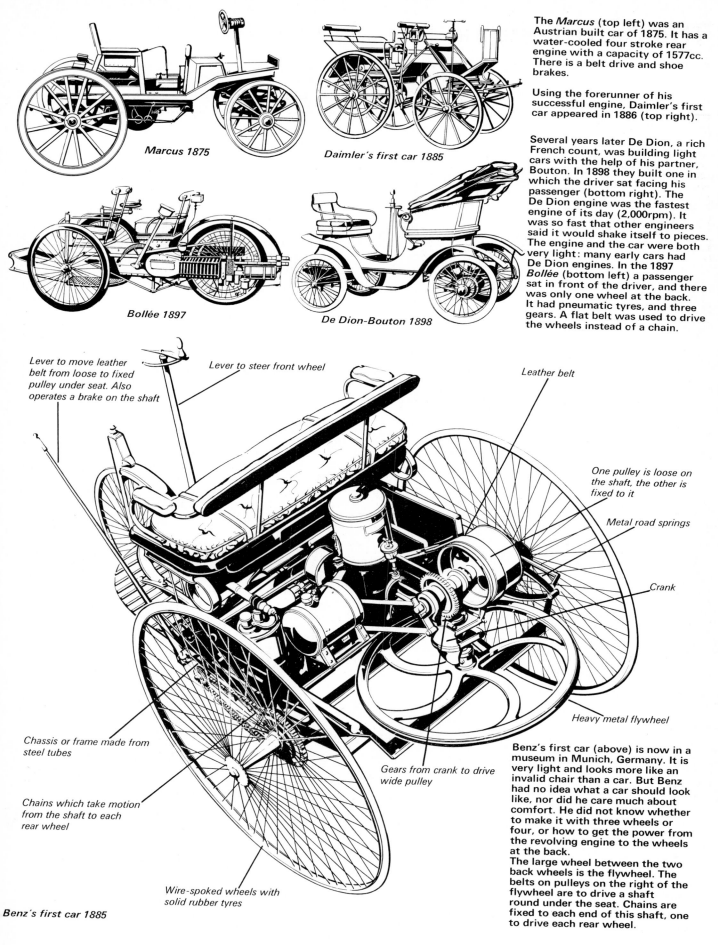

Marcus 1875

Daimler's first car 1885

Bollée 1897

De Dion-Bouton 1898

The *Marcus* (top left) was an Austrian built car of 1875. It has a water-cooled four stroke rear engine with a capacity of 1577cc. There is a belt drive and shoe brakes.

Using the forerunner of his successful engine, Daimler's first car appeared in 1886 (top right).

Several years later De Dion, a rich French count, was building light cars with the help of his partner, Bouton. In 1898 they built one in which the driver sat facing his passenger (bottom right). The De Dion engine was the fastest engine of its day (2,000rpm). It was so fast that other engineers said it would shake itself to pieces. The engine and the car were both very light: many early cars had De Dion engines. In the 1897 *Bollée* (bottom left) a passenger sat in front of the driver, and there was only one wheel at the back. It had pneumatic tyres, and three gears. A flat belt was used to drive the wheels instead of a chain.

Lever to move leather belt from loose to fixed pulley under seat. Also operates a brake on the shaft

Lever to steer front wheel

Leather belt

One pulley is loose on the shaft, the other is fixed to it

Metal road springs

Crank

Heavy metal flywheel

Chassis or frame made from steel tubes

Chains which take motion from the shaft to each rear wheel

Gears from crank to drive wide pulley

Wire-spoked wheels with solid rubber tyres

Benz's first car 1885

Benz's first car (above) is now in a museum in Munich, Germany. It is very light and looks more like an invalid chair than a car. But Benz had no idea what a car should look like, nor did he care much about comfort. He did not know whether to make it with three wheels or four, or how to get the power from the revolving engine to the wheels at the back.
The large wheel between the two back wheels is the flywheel. The belts on pulleys on the right of the flywheel are to drive a shaft round under the seat. Chains are fixed to each end of this shaft, one to drive each rear wheel.

5

The race for speed 1894–1905

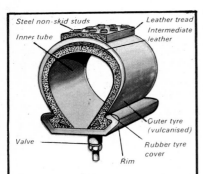

Early pneumatic tyre

The very first cars had wooden wheels with iron tyres. Then came solid rubber tyres, which were not so noisy and did not skid on the roads. Finally, the pneumatic tyre (above) was made. Cars with pneumatic tyres could go faster and were more comfortable. Dunlop, an Irish vet, and the French Michelin brothers both experimented with pneumatic car tyres in the 1890s. The first pneumatic tyres were not very reliable. One of the first cars to run on them was entered by Michelin in the 1895 race. No one knows how many punctures had to be repaired but 22 new inner tubes were used. It was some years before this type of tyre was used by everyone.

Many of the cars in the first road races failed to finish and of those that did some were only able to do so because of the drivers' skill. One 1902 *Renault* (right) however, looked as if it was built for speed. Marcel Renault won the light car section of a 620-mile race in it at an average speed of nearly 40mph.

Designers made faster cars by making bigger, more powerful engines. This led to more modern-looking cars. Jenatzy won the 327-mile Gordon Bennett Cup race in a *Mercedes* car (right) at an average speed of nearly 50mph. With such high speeds, it is not surprising that there was trouble. Spectators were not controlled and dogs, horses, cattle and people wandered all over the roads. In the 1903 Paris-Madrid race Louis Renault ran over four dogs, and his brother, Marcel, was killed. Newspapers called it the 'race of death', and it was stopped at Bordeaux, the cars being sent back to Paris by train. Gabriel in a *Mors* had averaged an incredible 65·3mph to Bordeaux, a speed few drivers could equal today. Now that there were fast, reliable cars, the next step was to make them easier to drive, safer and more comfortable.

Road races

The early inventors and engineers wanted to show people that motor cars were reliable and fast. So races were held to try to get the public interested in cars. The races were run on roads, as rallies are today, and race tracks were not used until later.

In July 1894, Giffard, the editor of a French newspaper, organised a race for horseless carriages over 79 miles of roads between Paris and Rouen. Thirteen cars took part in the trial. The race was won by the Comte de Dion in his steam car at an average speed of 11·6mph. Racing could be fun, and it did rouse public interest, but it could be dangerous. Levassor had a very bad accident when his car collided with a dog, and he died soon afterwards.

Finding faults

All the time the drivers were learning more about their vehicles. They discovered what happened to the cars when they were driven over long distances at maximum speed in all weathers. They found that many parts were not good enough, and it was up to the makers and the inventors to think of new ideas to make the cars more reliable and go still faster.

Marcel Renault in the 1902 Paris-Vienna Race

Mercedes 1903

Wire wheels with pneumatic tyres

Steering by lever or tiller

Box for tools and spare parts

Candle lamps

Peugeot 1896

The *Peugeot* (left) took part in races in 1896. Like many of the petrol cars at that time, it still had the shape of the light horse-drawn carriages. A small engine was placed under the seat and the driver and passenger sat high up in the car.

Although the *Peugeot* had pneumatic tyres and good springs, the brakes were not very good and the steering was hard to control. All the shocks from bumps on the roads came up the steering column to the tiller bar. There was no steering wheel, and the driver had to hold the tiller very tightly to stop it jumping out of his hands. This was difficult when changing gear, and operating all the levers. Little could be done to make cars like this go very much faster. New ideas were still needed.

Panhard and Levassor 1895

The 1894 race was so successful that in the following year the first French Grand Prix was run. It ran for 732 miles, from Paris to Bordeaux and back again. Eighteen vehicles set off and the first one back was a *Panhard and Levassor* (left), driven by the inventor Emile Levassor. He drove all the way himself for more than 48 hours, with only a few very short stops. His car had a two-cylinder petrol engine and solid rubber tyres and reached a top speed of only 18mph on a flat road. The average speed was 15mph.

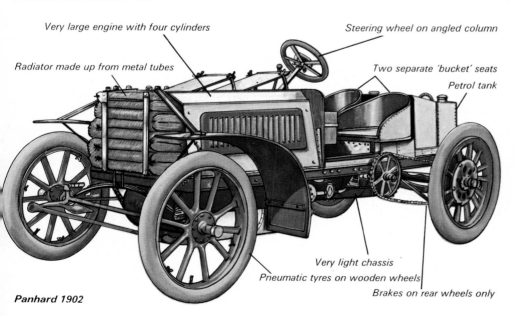

Very large engine with four cylinders

Steering wheel on angled column

Radiator made up from metal tubes

Two separate 'bucket' seats

Petrol tank

Very light chassis

Pneumatic tyres on wooden wheels

Brakes on rear wheels only

Panhard 1902

In 1902 the *Panhard* (left), driven by Charles Jarrott, won the Circuit of Ardennes in Belgium at 54mph.

The engine, which takes up more space than anything else, is at the front, as it is in most modern cars. The drive is fed to the rear wheels by chains, and through a gearbox under the seats.

The wooden wheels and chassis had to be much stronger to carry the weight, yet this was one of the lightest racing cars made at the time. Comfort was still not very important in racing cars, and the drivers had to be strong, as well as brave. The roads were made up only from stones and earth. Thousands of horses were still being used, and they made the road surface even rougher.

Brakes have had to be improved as the speed of the cars has increased. In the first type, a metal 'spoon' was pressed against the solid rubber tyre. On faster cars with pneumatic tyres, firstly contracting bands and later expanding shoes lined with asbestos were forced out to come into contact with a metal drum at the centre of the two rear wheels. By the mid-1920s, four wheel braking was common on most European cars: American cars held out to the end of the decade.

In the 1960s disc brakes were put onto the front wheels. Pads are forced against a disc at the centre of the wheel. Disc brakes are used on many modern cars.

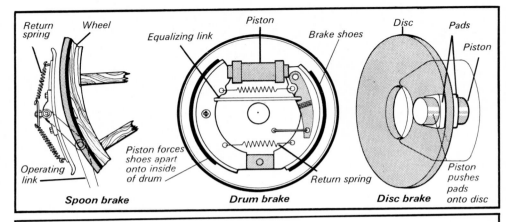

Spoon brake   **Drum brake**   **Disc brake**

Factory machinery was driven at one time by flat leather belts. The idea was copied in the first cars, but leather belts slipped on the metal pulleys so they were replaced by a chain on each wheel. The chains were the same as those used on bicycles, but much larger and stronger. Nevertheless, they often broke and were difficult to repair.

When car engines were placed at the front, the power had to reach the rear wheels. This was done by a metal tube called a propeller shaft. The shaft was turned by the engine and the motion was transmitted to each back wheel via the back axle. This method of transmission is over 70 years old and is still used in a number of cars today.

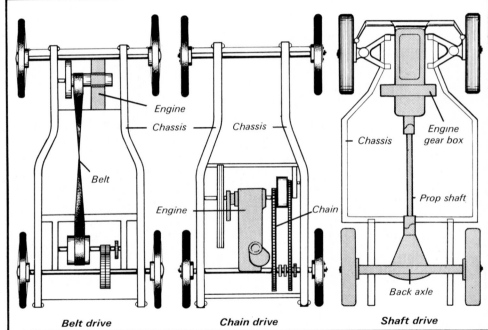

Belt drive   **Chain drive**   **Shaft drive**

Good suspension is essential for both comfort and roadholding. In horse-drawn vehicles the body was held between long arms which were part of the chassis. It swayed around, but it was better to have leather straps than to have the body fixed direct to the chassis. Front and rear axles, which hold the wheels, were fixed to the chassis by long metal springs made up of several leaves. They were all bolted together in the centre and were very strong. This type of spring is still used on some cars today, but most of them use coil springs. The coil is held upright by metal plates and rods and partly compressed before it is put in position.

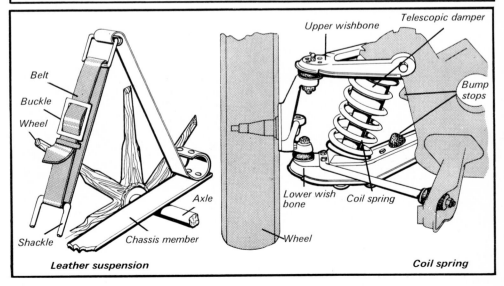

Leather suspension   **Coil spring**

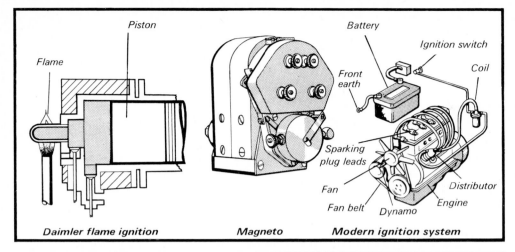

Flame | Piston | Battery | Ignition switch | Coil | Front earth | Sparking plug leads | Fan | Fan belt | Dynamo | Distributor | Engine

Daimler flame ignition | **Magneto** | **Modern ignition system**

The purpose of an ignition system is to provide intense heat. This explodes the compressed mixture of petrol vapour and air in the cylinder to provide the power stroke. In the first engines this was done by heating up a piece of platinum metal. One end was inside the cylinder and was heated by a spirit lamp outside.

Next came an electric spark which was made by a machine called a magneto. High voltage electricity was produced when the magneto was turned and taken by a wire to a sparking plug. A spark ignited the mixture.

Magnetos were replaced by the modern ignition system in the 1920s. This gets an electric spark from a battery and a coil and passes the current to each plug through a distributor.

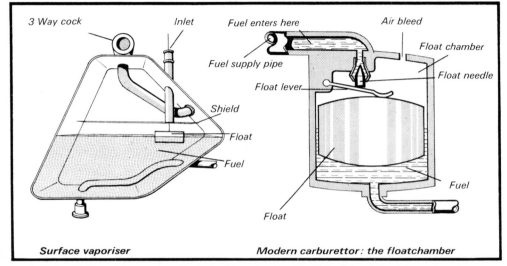

3 Way cock | Inlet | Fuel enters here | Air bleed | Float chamber | Float needle | Fuel supply pipe | Float lever | Shield | Float | Fuel | Fuel | Float

Surface vaporiser | **Modern carburettor: the floatchamber**

Petrol vapour must be mixed with the correct amount of air to make an explosive mixture. In the 1890s a surface vaporiser was used. The petrol was heated by a tube filled with hot water from the cooling system of the engine. Vapour from the warm fuel was mixed with air and the mixture entered the cylinder through a valve.

Shortly after, the carburettor was invented to do the same job. Petrol is kept at a certain level by a float in the carburettor bowl. As the engine valve opens and the piston goes down the cylinder, air is drawn across the jet. Petrol spray comes out of the jet and mixes with the air to give the correct mixture. The speed at which it enters the cylinder is controlled by a throttle valve which in turn is joined up to the accelerator pedal.

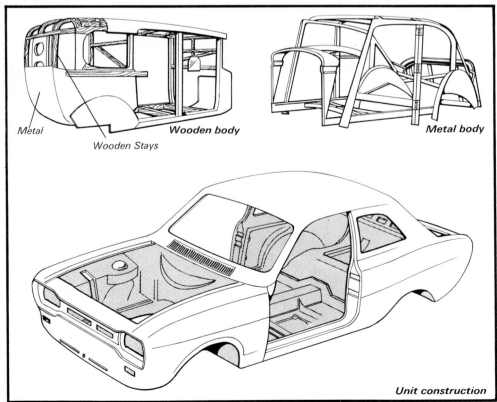

Metal | Wooden Stays | **Wooden body** | **Metal body**

Unit construction

The chassis and body of early cars were built quite separately and put together at the end. Engineers made the chassis and the working parts of the car, and coach-builders, who had worked on horse-drawn carriages, built the body.

Bodies had a wooden framework covered with thin metal panels. By 1930 body frames were made from metal instead of wood. They were still separate from the chassis and held to it by nuts and bolts.

Since the late 1930s a new type of car building, called unit construction, has been used. The separate parts of the body and chassis are welded together to make a metal box. Cars can now be made more quickly and cheaply and the finished shell is very strong.

Motoring for gentlemen car sales until 1914

Supply and demand

Road trials and the Continental races had persuaded people to accept the car. German inventors had worked out how to make cars go, and the French had taken up the idea and were beginning to make cars to sell in bigger and bigger numbers. Up to 1900 probably 4,000 motor cars had been sold. By 1913 dozens of manufacturers were producing more than 1,000 cars a year.

Most of the cars were for gentlemen: only the rich could afford to buy and run a car. A manufacturer can only sell if he makes things that are needed or wanted. This is called supplying for the demand. The greatest demand was for the gentleman's carriage, so that is what was made. Cars no longer looked like horse carriages with engines. Now the engine was at the front under a bonnet, with a radiator in front of it and a dashboard behind. Drivers and rear passengers sat in separate compartments in a wood and metal body made by the most skilled craftsmen.

By 1913 almost everyone with enough money owned a car. In America a man called Henry Ford had different ideas—cheaper cars for everybody.

Peugeot 1905

The King of Portugal drove a *Peugeot* in 1905 (above). There was no glass windscreen to protect him from wind and rain, so he wore a long waterproof coat. Most people also wore goggles to keep the dust out of their eyes. The front and back parts of the body were still separate, and the front did not have doors. The passengers got into the rear by standing on the running board and then on to the other little step. The large hood at the back could be raised in bad weather, but it did not stop the rain blowing in at the sides and at the front.

Benz 1907

By 1907, *Benz* cars (above) were much bigger than the first one made twenty years before. They still looked like the *Peugeot,* as did most cars made for the rich at that time. The 1907 *Benz* did have a glass windscreen, however. By this time, they also all have pneumatic tyres except in rural America. A bulb horn was fitted to the steering column. The top part of the shiny brass radiator at the front of the engine is also visible. This car could go faster than 60mph.

Austin Landaulet 1911

Rear compartment for five passengers

Speaking-tube

Removable leather hood

Cloth upholstery

Separate chairs

Body and chassis still two separate parts

Leather upholstery

Motoring Accessories from a catalogue of 1909.

The *'Contessa' Motoring Hood* described as the latest idea in ladies headwear. 'In best quality Silk or Crepe de Chine, with Lace Veil and Mica front.' (Right).

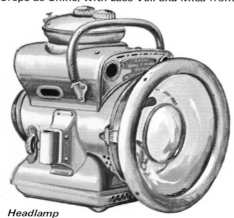

Headlamp

This splendid headlamp was called the *'King of the Road'*. It was made of brass and stood 12" high. It burnt acetylene gas. (Above).

Ladies' hood

Man's travelling cap

(Below) The *'Multi-twist'* was described as 'A very handsome production'. Its multi-spiral form gives a deep rich cornet note; loud, prolonged and effective.

Motor horn

This *'Travelling Cap'* is one of *'Dr. Jaeger's Specialities in Hats and Caps'*. 'It is fleecy knitted, and very warm and comfortable.' (Left).

Luggage space on roof

Windscreen which could be opened

Separate compartment for the chauffeur

Oil side lamps

Acetylene headlamps

Running board to act as a step

Large tool box

In the early 1900s, *Austin* cars were often fitted with a three-quarter *Landaulet* body (left). In 1911, the body alone cost £225. Such high quality coachwork gave the wealthy car owners the same standards of comfort as they would expect in their drawing rooms. The paid driver sat in his own part of the car, while the owner gave directions from the back through a speaking-tube.

Fiat 1914

The 1914 Italian *Fiat* (above) had electric lights and a windscreen. It is an example of a touring car with four doors. The shape of the body, like the *Mercedes*, looks as if it is made from one piece of metal. It was longer and thinner than earlier cars, and was called a Torpedo body. The front part is no longer separated from the back, so the driver felt he was in the same car as his passengers. Many car owners enjoyed driving, so did not use chauffeurs.

Mercedes 1914

In the big 1914 *Mercedes* (above), the old oil lamps at the side have gone, and large electric lamps are put at the side of the radiator instead of the acetylene gas lights.
The bodywork has now become enclosed. Even the wings look as if they are a part of the body. The bonnet. scuttle and body are in line as if they were made in one piece. The back part of the body is for the passengers and is waterproof. The front door is on the driver's side.

The first popular car the Model 'T' Ford

Henry Ford was the first man to make motoring possible for almost everybody in America. He did it with his *Model 'T'* car. His slogan was 'reliability and low cost'. The name Ford has been famous ever since.

Record sales

When the last *Model 'T' Ford* was produced, in 1927, 15 million of them had been sold. The only other car to be manufactured in anything like the same number was the German-made *Volkswagen*.

Henry Ford was born in America in 1863. His father was an Irishman who had gone to America to be a farmer. Henry wanted to be a mechanic, so when he left school at 16 he went to work in a small factory. Later he repaired farm steam engines. The unsuccessful tractor he built, in the 1880s, was driven by steam. In 1896

he had made his first petrol car, and in 1899 gave up his job to form his own company.

Mass production pioneer

The first *Model 'T'* was made in 1908, and it was the first car to be built by modern mass production methods. While the price of most cars went up each year (and still does), the *Model 'T'* actually went down. In 1927 it cost only a third of the price of the same car in 1908. No major change in its design was made in all those years. People called it the 'Tin Lizzie', but this did not stop them from buying it—and loving it.

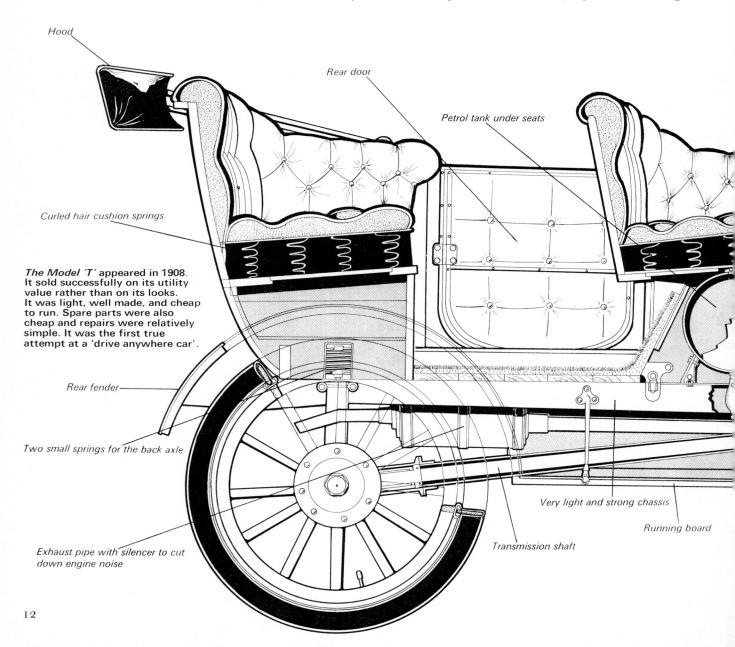

Hood

Rear door

Petrol tank under seats

Curled hair cushion springs

The Model 'T' appeared in 1908. It sold successfully on its utility value rather than on its looks. It was light, well made, and cheap to run. Spare parts were also cheap and repairs were relatively simple. It was the first true attempt at a 'drive anywhere car'.

Rear fender

Two small springs for the back axle

Very light and strong chassis

Running board

Transmission shaft

Exhaust pipe with silencer to cut down engine noise

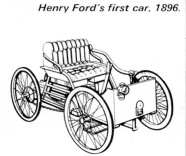

Henry Ford's first car was built in 1896 and was described by him as a quadricycle. It was powered by a twin-cylinder four stroke engine mounted at the rear. The car's weight was only 4½cwt and it ran for 25 miles on a tankful of petrol.

Henry Ford's first workshop at 58 Bagley Avenue, Detroit, US. 1896 (left).

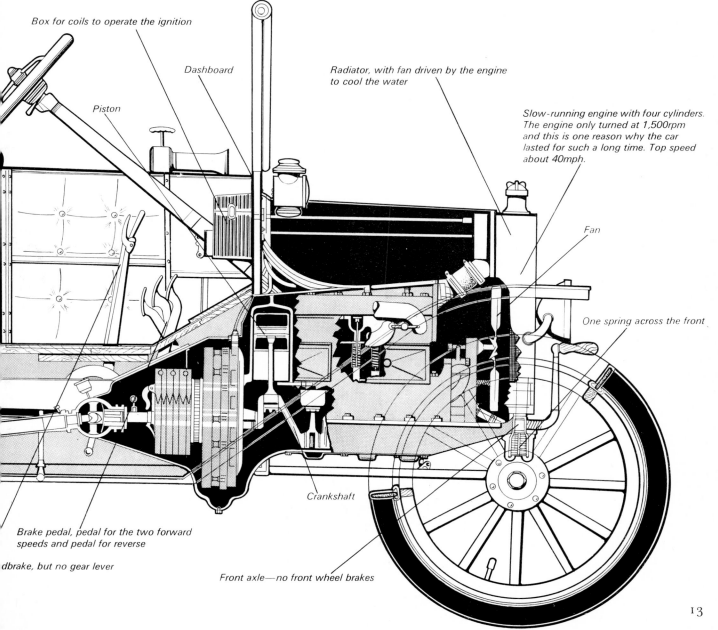

Box for coils to operate the ignition

Dashboard

Piston

Radiator, with fan driven by the engine to cool the water

Slow-running engine with four cylinders. The engine only turned at 1,500rpm and this is one reason why the car lasted for such a long time. Top speed about 40mph.

Fan

One spring across the front

Crankshaft

Brake pedal, pedal for the two forward speeds and pedal for reverse

dbrake, but no gear lever

Front axle—no front wheel brakes

The motoring craze in the 1920s

In the very early days motorists got their petrol from chemists. As more and more cars were used, the sale of petrol became the job of the local ironmonger. He sold the petrol in 2 gallon cans. Motorists who ran out of petrol at night were stranded until the morning. The first roadside petrol pumps began to appear in the early twenties.

Morris at early petrol pump

Some of the light, cheap cars made in France (right), could travel more than 40 miles on one gallon of petrol, but they could not go very fast. There are no brakes on the front wheels. Cars with brakes on all four wheels are much safer but were not used on many cars until 1925. By 1920, most cars had electric lamps worked from a battery. Almost all the cars were open with hoods and were called tourers. They also had side screens that fitted into the tops of the doors and kept out most of the wind and rain.

Peugeot Quadrilette 1920

The *Rolls-Royce* (right) was one of the best and most expensive cars in the world. They are still made today, but they look much more modern. They had large engines and were very powerful. People who had enough money to buy them did not worry about how much petrol they used. They wanted comfort, power and silence, and they did not mind how much they paid. *Rolls-Royce* cars were so quiet that one model was called the *Silver Ghost*.

Rolls-Royce coupé 1927

Bean cars (right) were made in Tipton, Dudley. In the twenties they became a very popular make. They were strong and reliable but heavy. Unlike the *Rolls-Royce* they were not made for the very rich. There were so many different carmakers in the twenties that it was not possible for them all to compete with those using mass production methods. *Bean* was one of the casualties.

Bean 1920

American exports

The First World War interrupted car production in Europe for three years from 1915 to 1918. As soon as the war was over more cars were wanted than ever before. Some people still wanted expensive luxury models, but thousands of cheap economy cars were needed too. Henry Ford had already discovered this new market with his cheap, fast-selling *Model 'T' Ford*. In fact, cars had to be imported from America into Europe. America thus became the first big car exporting country in the world.

Mass production in Europe

Imported cars solved the problem in Britain for a while, but it was obviously cheaper to manufacture the cars in the country where they were to be sold. Although the war had put a temporary stop to cars, it was to lead to a revolution in car production. During the war factory owners and engineers had to find ways of mass producing arms. After the war, some of the factories started to make cars again. The engineers adapted their ideas for fast production, and cars went into mass production.

Both Austin and Morris produced successful cars by these methods in the twenties. The secret of Austin's success was the small *Austin Seven*. In France, Italy, and Germany too, the trend was to producing cars cheap enough for the 'ordinary' people.

Of course, not all cars were mass produced. Many were still made by hand in small factories. In Europe there were many different makes of car—like the luxurious *Hispano-Suiza* and *Isotta-Fraschini*. There famous names were to disappear as mass production increased.

Car buyers wanted cars that were cheap to run as well as buy. This meant that the cars should not use much petrol. In America, petrol consumption has never been a problem, because petrol is cheap. In Europe, oil has to be imported so petrol is expensive. Most small cars have a lower petrol consumption than big ones, so they became very popular in Europe.

The car producing countries of the world made $3\frac{1}{2}$ million cars in 1924. By 1929 they were making over 5 million each year. Most of them were cheap cars for ordinary families.

Essex saloon 1922

The *Essex* (left) was the first cheap saloon car to be made in America. The passengers all sat under cover and were much more comfortable than they would be in a tourer on a wet, windy day. If they wanted more fresh air on a hot day, they could open the windscreen.

Saloon bodies like this became more and more popular, and by about 1928 there were more saloons than tourers built each year. The body of this *Essex* was made from steel, but some cars had bodies made from stiff cloth called fabric. Very few European cars had wooden wheels after 1922, although they were used in America into the 1930s.

Austin 7 1928

Herbert Austin, a British car manufacturer who became a lord, made the first successful baby car in Europe in 1922. All the mechanical parts were made in his own factory. These cheap little cars made motoring possible for everybody. The 1928 saloon model (left) cost £150 and it did not cost much more than $\frac{1}{2}$p a mile to run. Although it looks very small, there was enough room for three children in the back.

Lancia Lambda 1925

The *Lancia Lambda* (left) could go at more than 70mph. It was an expensive Italian car. Most 1920s cars still had running boards which acted as steps for getting in and out. Wheels were large and the seats were quite high up in the bodies. The *Lambda* pioneered unit body chassis construction. Streamlining was not yet an acceptable feature of cars. The radiators and the lights, for instance, were not fitted into the shape of the body, and the front and rear wings were separate from the rest of the body. Spare wheels were carried outside, either at the back or fixed on to the running board.

Cars and people

The magazine Punch has always produced cartoons which tell how people are learning to live with the car. Here is a selection which appeared between 1900 and 1940. In the early days of motoring, most road users rode horses and bicycles.

In winter, the roads were almost always covered with mud. In summer it was very dusty. The first cars were slow, noisy, and unreliable. With solid tyres their steering was often clumsy. It is easy to imagine the passing of such a car shattering the peace of the countryside. Horses were scared and often bolted at the sight of a car. The cartoonist's comparison on the right is very apt. Horse users really hated cars. Sometimes they even whipped the motorist as he passed by.

BROTHERS IN ADVERSITY
Farmer: 'Pull up, you fool! the mare's bolting!'
Motorist: 'So's the car!'

Driving through the country was dangerous. The motorist had to make his way through straying chickens and to fight off barking dogs. Pedestrians were un-accustomed to motor cars. Even at this early stage we see the motorist beginning to think that he owns the road. This cartoon (right) ably shows the sort of scene where the term 'road hog' might have been first used.

Motor Fiend: 'Why don't you get out of the way?'
Victim: 'What! are you coming back?'

For sometime still, a breakdown could be expected on almost every journey. As in our cartoon (right), the owner—or more often his chauffeur/mechanic usually finished up on his back under the car. A parked motor car always attracted attention. Passers-by would stop and make comments and usually unfriendly ones at that. Sometimes quite large crowds gathered. Cars were still regarded by most people as playthings of the rich. They made their resentment clear.

'It's stopped rainin', mister.'

The Austin Seven of the 1920s
was so small compared with other
makes that it was soon known as
the 'baby'. To many people it was
just like having an extra member of
the family. Owners of big cars
were always ready to laugh at
jokes about people who owned
small ones (left).

I can't come out yet, Dear: 'I'm washing the baby.'

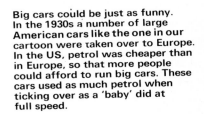

Big cars could be just as funny.
In the 1930s a number of large
American cars like the one in our
cartoon were taken over to Europe.
In the US, petrol was cheaper than
in Europe, so that more people
could afford to run big cars. These
cars used as much petrol when
ticking over as a 'baby' did at
full speed.

'D'you mind switching off, Sir? She's gaining on me.'

People may have laughed at small
cars, but Europe could not have
done without them. It was the
only way to produce cars cheap
enough for the ordinary people.
They were regarded as toys,
ashtrays and so on—but people
bought them in their thousands.
Today many Americans are finding
small imported cars more practical.
Just as in Europe, 40 years ago,
fun is made of small cars, but
people are buying them.

The Driver: 'What do you think of those little things?'
The Passenger: 'Make topping ash-trays.'

Racing in the 20's and 30's

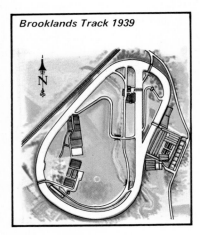

Brooklands Track 1939

Brooklands Course in Surrey, England (above) was the first circuit in the world to be built specially for car racing, as long ago as 1907. Similar ones were made in America, France and Italy. These large circuits were made of concrete, and banked curves were used on the corners. Such circuits are ideal for testing cars as well as for racing.

Maximum speeds round the 2·8-mile Brooklands Course increased steadily from 1922 to 1935.

1922—123mph
1924—128mph
1925—129mph
1928—131mph
1929—134mph
1930—135mph
1932—137mph
1934—140mph
1935—143mph

In 1935, John Cobb drove a *Napier-Railton* car at an average speed of nearly 152mph over half a mile. This was the highest speed ever recorded at Brooklands.

The 1924 Type 35 *Bugatti* (right), with an 8-cylinder engine, was the most successful racing car of all time. Yet some of the *Bugatti* models could be used on the roads as ordinary cars as, unlike most other racing cars, they could be fitted with lights, wings and a hood.

Ettore Bugatti, who finished his first car in 1909, was a brilliant designer. Every part of any car he sold was made with the same precision as the smallest part of a watch. There are still a number of his cars left today. Some are in museums, but some people still race them in special events for vintage cars.

Racing at Brooklands 1920s

The testing sport

From the very early days of motoring racing has been very important for two reasons. As a sport, it has tested the skill and daring of the drivers, and given enjoyment to thousands of spectators. Apart from that, racing has tested the cars themselves. The high speeds meant that the cars and engines had to work much harder than if they had been used for normal motoring. If parts were weak or badly designed, motor racing soon found them out.

Experimental prototypes were also tried out in racing. Four-wheel brakes were first tested on racing cars, and within a few years every ordinary car had them. New wheel and tyre designs were put through the same tough tests. Race tracks were built all over the world from about 1910, because of the high rate of bad crashes in the early road races.

Once cars became safer, road racing started again on the Continent, but over sections that were closed to the public. Now, cars are made specifically for racing and for breaking speed records. Race tracks remained popular and thousands of people went to watch while bets were placed on drivers and cars rather like at horse races.

Bugatti 1924

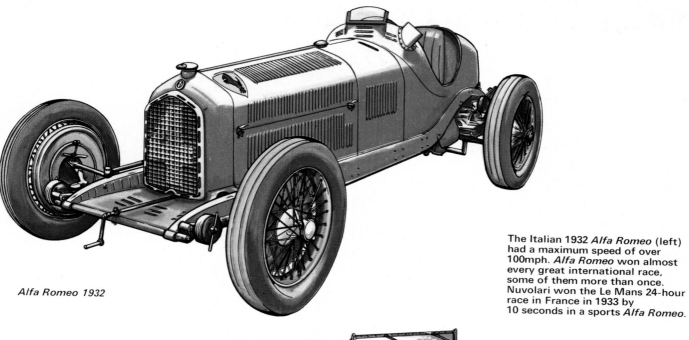

Alfa Romeo 1932

The Italian 1932 *Alfa Romeo* (left) had a maximum speed of over 100mph. *Alfa Romeo* won almost every great international race, some of them more than once. Nuvolari won the Le Mans 24-hour race in France in 1933 by 10 seconds in a sports *Alfa Romeo*.

This British car is a 4½-litre *Bentley* (right). In Europe, engine capacity is measured in cubic centimetres and is calculated on the area swept by the pistons. In the U.S. the size is measured in cubic inches.

Bentley 1929

Auto-Union 1938

The 1938 3-litre German *Auto-Union* (left) was a real racing car. The huge 12-cylinder engine was fitted behind the driver's seat—the short ends of six of the exhaust pipes are visible at the side. This supercharged 500 horse-power car won the 1938 Italian Grand Prix in the hands of Tazio Nuvolari.

Mass production the assembly line

This diagram below is of a typical modern assembly line. Each firm's line differs in small ways. In all firms a lot of the parts are made in other factories. Sometimes, as with tyres, they are made by a completely different company. The diagram represents a continuous flow from left to right. The process starts in the Press shop. The big machines are very noisy. They press the sheet steel into shape to make boots, bonnets, wings, and other pieces for the car bodies. The biggest presses have a pressure of 2,000 tons.

Machine-built cars

Car bodies are pressed out of a sheet of steel with one blow from a huge machine called a press. This gives the body all its shapes, and cuts out all the spaces for the doors and the windows. Quick-drying paint is sprayed on from a spray-gun and the whole thing can be done in a few hours. Some small parts are just dipped in a large tub of paint and passed through a hot oven to dry.

Final assembly

Mass production of modern cars is done by making machines do most of the work. Machines are accurate and can do the work much quicker than men. But there are still a lot of people working in a factory. Skilled workers are needed to control the machines.

Some jobs cannot be done by machines at all. Joining all the parts of a car together is called final assembly. This is done by men. The finished parts all arrive at the entrance of a very long workshop. A number of flat moving tracks, like escalators in shops and underground stations, carry the car along. Every few yards a man stands holding the next part to be fitted. As the track moves along, he fits his part and waits for the next car. The one he

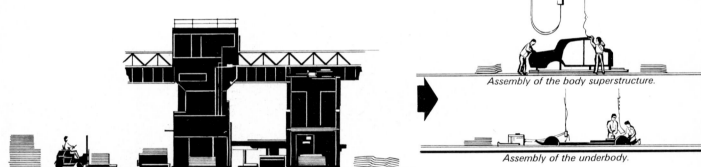

Assembly of the body superstructure.

Assembly of the underbody.

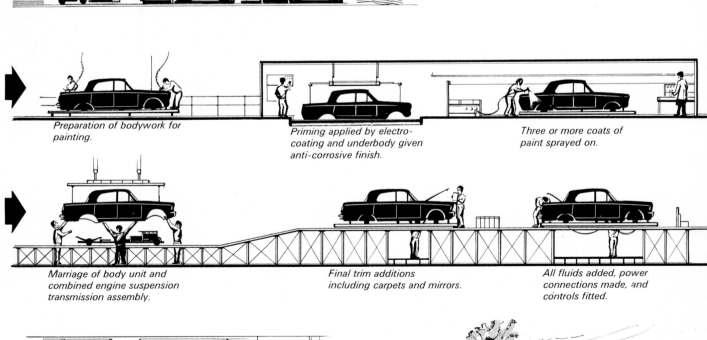

Preparation of bodywork for painting.

Priming applied by electro-coating and underbody given anti-corrosive finish.

Three or more coats of paint sprayed on.

Marriage of body unit and combined engine suspension transmission assembly.

Final trim additions including carpets and mirrors.

All fluids added, power connections made, and controls fitted.

Car is driven to roller testing station. Testing of mechanical parts and electrical circuits.

Short road test.

Workers on the assembly line (right) complete work on the body shell. Both men and women do this work. There are several assembly lines running parallel to each other along the factory.

has just done goes on to the next man, who fits a different part.

Everyone must be accurate and quick. There cannot be any mistakes, and if a part is missed it may not be possible to fit the next part. The track has to be stopped and that means that everybody has to stop working until it is running again. There may be a thousand men working on the track. The men work in shifts: some start at night and have to sleep during the day.

Welding together of super-structure and underbody.

Addition of doors, bonnet and boot covers.

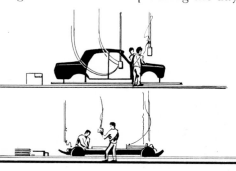

Drying in heated ovens.

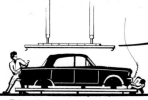

Trim shop where hundreds of parts added. These include grill, electrical wiring, lights, windscreen, windows.

Casting of engine block and cylinder head. Assembly and checking of engine, engine parts, gearbox. Marriage of gearbox and engine. Bolting together of all the engine, transmission, and suspension elements.

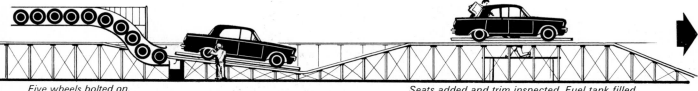

Five wheels bolted on.

Seats added and trim inspected. Fuel tank filled.

The Water Test—high pressure bombardment to check for leaks. Final inspection.

Dispatched to trade lines to await delivery.

The family car

Ford 1939

In 1935 Ford in Britain brought out a car that the average family could afford. With its 8hp engine it could average 40mpg and reach 60mph. It was also cheap to maintain.

Age of the 'tin box'

By about 1930 most of the small car firms had either been bought by the bigger ones or had gone out of business. Many people were unemployed and there was not much money about. Most countries, in fact, were short of money in this period—known as the depression, or the slump. People naturally cut down on luxuries, so manufacturers concentrated on producing cheap cars.

The outside measurements of the cars in the 'tin box' age were kept as small as possible to save metal, and the bodies were made as big as possible within the frame. This may have been cheap, but it did not provide much comfort. The rear passengers, for instance, often had to sit right over the back wheels.

Evolution of the modern car

Advances in design were generally restricted to technical details, and little attention was paid to improving the looks of cars. Bodies became lower and new types of suspension were devised. Both features aided road-holding and facilitated a smoother ride. Streamlining and higher gear ratios made more speed possible. By 1939 the essentials of today's family saloon were in evidence.

American cars were still much larger than those made in Europe. The first *Plymouth* was made in Detroit in 1928. It was produced by an American called Walter Chrysler. By 1934 he had made a million *Plymouth* cars. The 1935 model (right) had the spare wheel on the side of the bonnet, while 1936 models had the spare at the rear.

From 1924, Chrysler also made cars under his own name. The Chrysler Corporation still makes *Chrysler, Imperial, Dodge* and *Plymouth* cars today. The French *Simca* and British Chrysler are also owned by the same company.

Plymouth PJ 1935

The *Austin* family cars were very popular. The firm still made the little *Austin Seven,* but the *Austin Ten* (right) was not very much more expensive and it had more room. In 1935 it cost £175. Herbert Austin made his first car, the *Wolseley,* in 1898, and he started his own factory in Birmingham in 1906. Austin, Morris and Ford made more cars than any other British firms in the 1930s. Austin and Morris were joined to form the British Motor Corporation in 1952. The Corporation now includes many famous names and is called British Leyland, although the old names are still used for the cars.

Austin Ten 'Lichfield' 1935

The changing shape of Dodge Cars 1914-1974

1914 Open tourer. Square lines. High seats. Running boards. Comfort not important.

1927 Tourer. The body is still high and square.

1937 Windscreen slopes back. Bumpers. Wings become part of the body. Body lower. Radiator shell and body curve.

1950 Windscreen slopes back even further. The running boards almost gone. The radiator shell, wings and head-lamps, moulded more into the body.

1960 No wings. Windscreen is curved round. Bonnet and boot same size.

1974 The modern car. There is little difference between front and back.

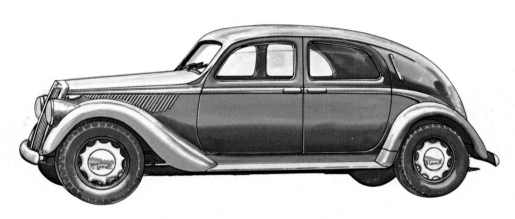

Lancia Aprilia 1939

Italian *Lancia* cars have always been different from other makes, and the designs were often ahead of the times. The *Aprilia* model used independent suspension, where each wheel is sprung separately instead of the wheel springs being connected. Cars with independent suspension can be more comfortable to drive, and are much safer because they have better roadholding. The car was also very low and streamlined so that there was less effect from the wind. Much of the engine was made of aluminium, which is a very light metal. It had a top speed of 80mph and a low petrol consumption of 28mpg.

Citroën 12, 1935

The *Citroën* was one of the most popular French family cars from 1919. The Traction Avant, shown here, was introduced in 1934. It was ahead of its time in two ways. The engine was in the front and drove straight on to the front wheels. The body was built up from pressed steel sections welded together in the form of a box. The same idea is used today. This type of body construction was stronger than that on many of the cars of the 1930s. Many of these *Citroëns* were used in France during the war, and a few are still in use.

The Beetle the incredible Volkswagen

Ferdinand Porsche was born in Austria, 1875. At 15 he was still only a tinsmith's apprentice but he soon showed a technical genius which earned him fame as a car designer. He shared Henry Ford's vision of a cheap car for the millions but could not convince the German manufacturers to sponsor him. Hitler was convinced, however, and with his backing Porsche went ahead.

The *Volkswagen 'Beetle'* has been as successful as the *Model 'T' Ford*. Like the Ford its basic shape has not altered since it was first made, although all the working parts have been redesigned to improve the car. Although it looks out of date, it is cheap and reliable and therefore very successful. Service and spare parts for the *Volkswagen* are available all over the world.

Ferdinand Porsche, a brilliant Austrian engineer, first thought of making a 'people's car' in the 1920s. Nobody was very interested in trying to help him at first. Three cars were made and tested in 1936. By 1938, Germans were offered the chance to start saving in advance for one of the new 'people's

cars'. Thousands of them did so. Work was started on a factory in Lower Saxony in May, 1938. The car was going to be called the *Kdf-Wagen*—the 'Strength-through-joy Car'. A year later, when only a few cars had been made, the war stopped production.

For the next four or five years the new factory made the *Kubelwagen* military jeeps and armaments. The factory was destroyed in the American air raids at the end of the war. Professor Heinz Nordhoff who took over the factory as a heap of rubble, built up a huge new factory which is now in its own town of Wolfsburg where 95,000 workers and their families live. The name *Volkswagen* means 'people's car'.

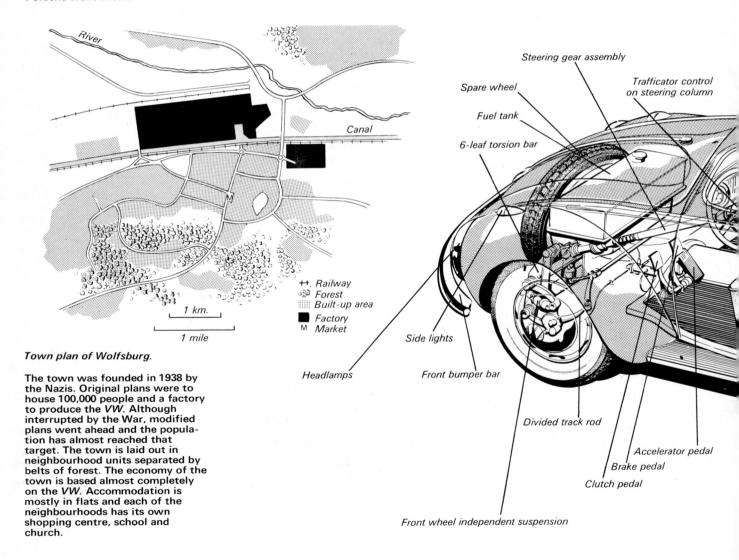

Town plan of Wolfsburg.

The town was founded in 1938 by the Nazis. Original plans were to house 100,000 people and a factory to produce the *VW*. Although interrupted by the War, modified plans went ahead and the population has almost reached that target. The town is laid out in neighbourhood units separated by belts of forest. The economy of the town is based almost completely on the *VW*. Accommodation is mostly in flats and each of the neighbourhoods has its own shopping centre, school and church.

24

The 1937 Volkswagen prototype

The first production models of the *Beetle* forerunner—the *Kdf-Wagen* were completed in 1939. With only 210 *Kdf-Wagens* finished Hitler ordered the new factory to switch to military vehicle production (above right). Production started up again with the encouragement of British Army officers in 1945.

The 1945 VW identical to the 1938 Kdf-Wagen.

A wartime product of the VW works—the amphibious Schwimmkübel

In that year nearly 1,800 *Volkswagens* were produced. Now they are produced at a rate of 5,000 every day. The basic design remains but of the 35,150 parts all but two have been changed or modified. During 1972 production exceeded 15 million, the previously unbeaten total held by the *Model 'T' Ford.*

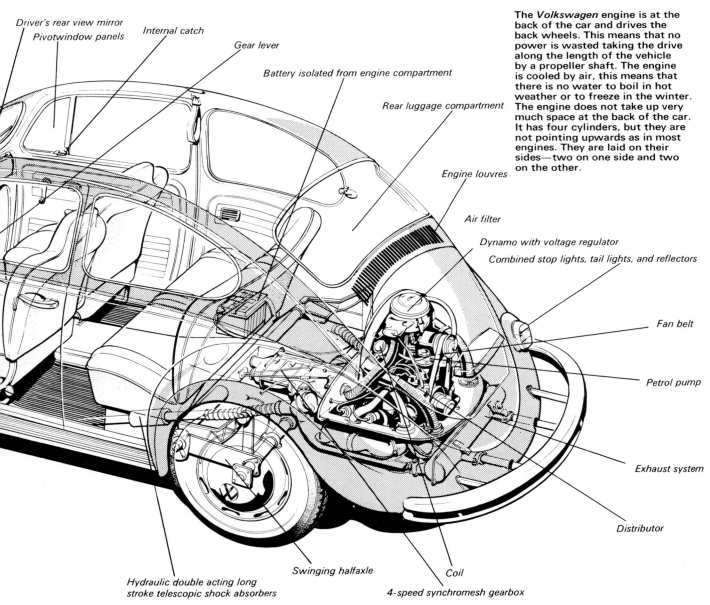

The *Volkswagen* engine is at the back of the car and drives the back wheels. This means that no power is wasted taking the drive along the length of the vehicle by a propeller shaft. The engine is cooled by air, this means that there is no water to boil in hot weather or to freeze in the winter. The engine does not take up very much space at the back of the car. It has four cylinders, but they are not pointing upwards as in most engines. They are laid on their sides—two on one side and two on the other.

Driver's rear view mirror

Pivotwindow panels

Internal catch

Gear lever

Battery isolated from engine compartment

Rear luggage compartment

Engine louvres

Air filter

Dynamo with voltage regulator

Combined stop lights, tail lights, and reflectors

Fan belt

Petrol pump

Exhaust system

Distributor

Coil

4-speed synchromesh gearbox

Swinging halfaxle

Hydraulic double acting long stroke telescopic shock absorbers

The Big Car Countries

population—203 million

U.S.A.

Ford Galaxie 500

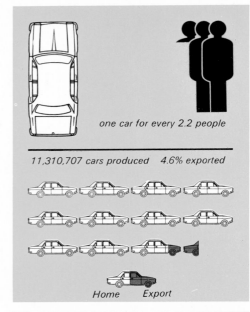

one car for every 2.2 people

11,310,707 cars produced   4.6% exported

Home   Export

The six main car producing countries of the world are shown on these pages. They make more cars in the United States than in any other country, and they have more cars than anywhere else. Some people measure how rich a country is by the number of people there are to each car in use. There is one car for every two people who live in Jersey. America is a very big country and people have to travel long journeys to work each day. The mother cannot do her shopping without a car, so she often has one of her own. Thus many families have at least two cars.

population—61 million

WEST GERMANY

BMW 3.0Si

one car for every 3.8 people

3,804,006 cars produced   57.3% exported

Home   Export

Since the war, which ended in 1945, the West German nation has become very prosperous. In 1968 they made the second highest number of cars in the world. They differ from the United States in that more than half the cars they make are sold to other countries. They are the world's greatest car exporters. Most of them are *Volkswagens*. The Americans export only four cars out of every hundred made. But they do either own or control their own factories all over the world. In Germany for example, they have Ford, and Opel (owned by General Motors).

population—103 million

JAPAN

Datsun Cherry

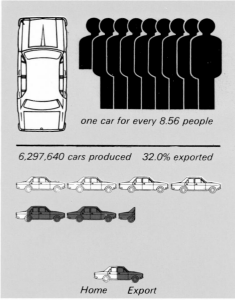

one car for every 8.56 people

6,297,640 cars produced   32.0% exported

Home   Export

There are still relatively few cars in use in Japan. And yet they are the second largest car making country. Only one in three is made for export, and that means that the Japanese people are getting cars themselves more quickly than in any other country. There are over eight people for every car in use, but this situation is changing fast. In 1946 only 110 cars were made in Japan, they reached $\frac{1}{2}$ million in 1964. They made four times that in 1968, and over twelve times that in 1972!

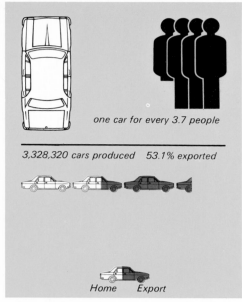

one car for every 3.7 people

3,328,320 cars produced   53.1% exported

Home   Export

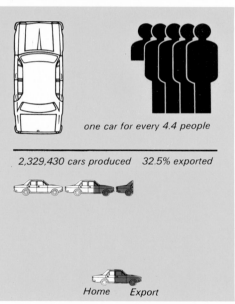

one car for every 4.4 people

2,329,430 cars produced   32.5% exported

Home   Export

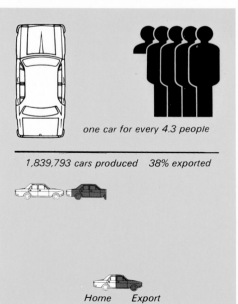

one car for every 4.3 people

1,839,793 cars produced   38% exported

Home   Export

population—51 million

FRANCE

Citroën GS

The French started with next to nothing in 1945. They made only 1,565 cars. By 1961 they were making more than Great Britain, and now there are more cars in France than anywhere else except America. They have also done very well with their exports. More than half of the cars made in 1972 were sold to other countries. Some countries have more strikes than others. If the workers in a car factory go on strike, the factory has to close down. All the people who are waiting for their new cars cannot get them. Sometimes they are not willing to wait and they buy other makes, or from another country.

population—55 million

GREAT BRITAIN

BLMC Mini Mk.2

Export or die applies to most car-making countries. Britain is no exception. Each year, just over a third of the cars are sent abroad. The value of all the goods connected with motoring adds up to a great amount each year. There are lorries, tractors, tyres, buses, spare parts being sold abroad by Britain for the huge sum of over £1000 million. More than 20,000 people work in a big car factory. Thousands more never see the factory, but get their work from the car industry. The delivery drivers, steel workers, salesmen and repair mechanics are some of them.

population—54 million

ITALY

Fiat 126

The biggest Italian firm is Fiat and their cars are popular everywhere. They make a very small, cheap model, as well as medium sized cars. Foreign cars are often more expensive to buy than cars made in the home country. This is because in many countries there are taxes on imports. In this way home sales are boosted.

Competition between the "Big Car Countries" has become very fierce. In Europe Britain and Italy are falling behind France and West Germany. Japan is still trying hard to increase exports, and they are already selling cars to many European countries.

27

General Motors the world's giant

General Motors cars through the years.

Olds experimental car 1897

V-16 Cadillac 1930

Chevrolet Bellair Sports Coupé 1960

Amalgamation

The motor industry is the most important industry in the Western World. It employs millions of people and earns countries more in exports than any other industry. As more cars are bought so the firms manufacturing them get bigger and bigger. The American General Motors Company is the biggest motor firm in the world, and employs more than three-quarters of a million people.

The beginnings of General Motors go back to when R. E. Olds built his first car in 1897. Six years later the Cadillac Company, and the Buick Motor Co. were formed. In 1907 the Oakland Motor Co. was founded in a town called Pontiac. An American, William C. Durant, joined the four firms together into one company in 1908.

In the motor industry, a large firm can be much more efficient than a number of small ones. Mass production can only work if many cars are being made, so if firms get together they can make cars more easily and more cheaply. This is called amalgamation. General Motors is the amalgamation of many firms, as you can see from the figures on the next page.

Reorganization and success

Durant was a clever man, but he was not very good at handling the huge business which he had created. He had good ideas and was a brilliant salesman, but he was a poor administrator. General Motors lost a lot of money in 1910 and again in 1920, so in 1923 Alfred Sloan took charge as the President. He soon found out what was going wrong. Unlike Henry Ford, General Motors were producing too many different models at different prices.

Sloan decided that the best thing to do was to improve the administration. The men at the top decided what the policy of the group should be, but left the day-to-day running of each section to the local management. A big company does not like to have to rely on other people for its parts. If the firm supplying sparking plugs cannot make enough, cars cannot be completed. So General Motors bought lots of these small firms, and they became part of the Group.

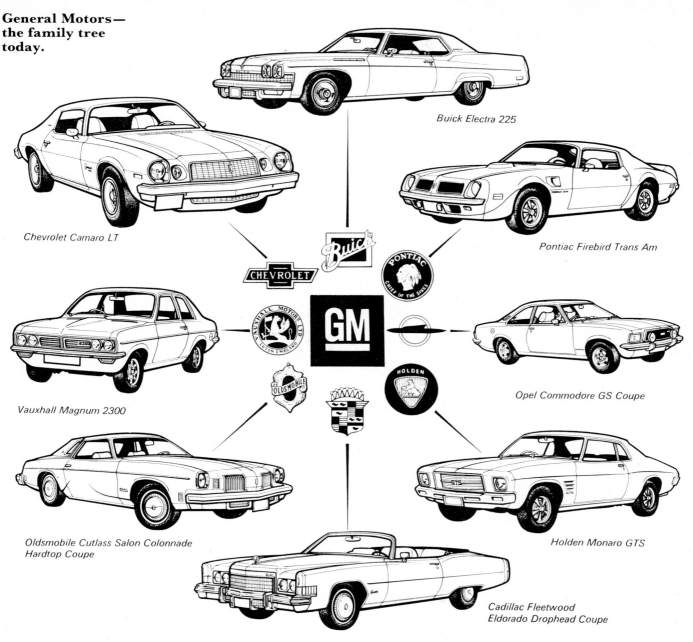

**General Motors—
the family tree
today.**

Buick Electra 225

Chevrolet Camaro LT

Pontiac Firebird Trans Am

Vauxhall Magnum 2300

Opel Commodore GS Coupe

Oldsmobile Cutlass Salon Colonnade
Hardtop Coupe

Holden Monaro GTS

Cadillac Fleetwood
Eldorado Drophead Coupe

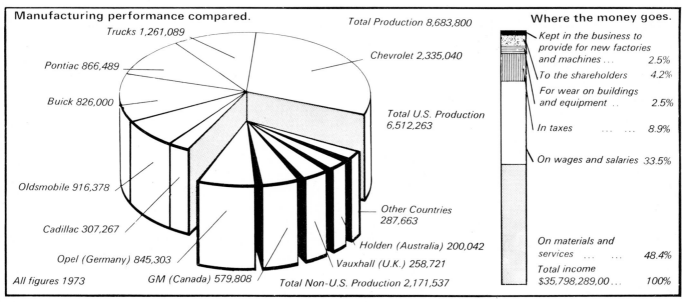

Manufacturing performance compared.

Total Production 8,683,800

Trucks 1,261,089

Pontiac 866,489

Buick 826,000

Chevrolet 2,335,040

Oldsmobile 916,378

Total U.S. Production
6,512,263

Cadillac 307,267

Opel (Germany) 845,303

Other Countries
287,663

Holden (Australia) 200,042

Vauxhall (U.K.) 258,721

GM (Canada) 579,808

Total Non-U.S. Production 2,171,537

All figures 1973

Where the money goes.

Kept in the business to
provide for new factories
and machines ...   2.5%

To the shareholders   4.2%

For wear on buildings
and equipment ...   2.5%

In taxes 8.9%

On wages and salaries 33.5%

On materials and
services 48.4%

Total income
$35,798,289,00 ...   100%

29

The sports car

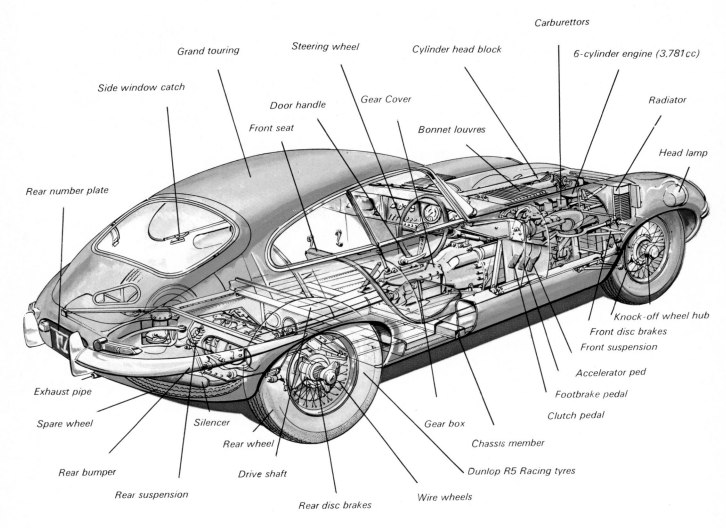

Carburettors

Grand touring Steering wheel Cylinder head block 6-cylinder engine (3,781 cc)

Side window catch Door handle Gear Cover Radiator

Front seat Bonnet louvres Head lamp

Rear number plate

Knock-off wheel hub
Front disc brakes
Front suspension

Accelerator ped

Footbrake pedal

Clutch pedal

Exhaust pipe

Spare wheel Silencer Gear box Chassis member

Rear wheel

Rear bumper Drive shaft Dunlop R5 Racing tyres

Rear suspension Wire wheels

Rear disc brakes

A famous name amongst sports cars is Britain's Jaguar. They are very fast, good to look at and reliable. The price is much lower than that of most other sports cars. For these reasons they are very popular and many are exported. This is the *'E' type Jaguar.* The first ones were made in 1961, and had a top speed of 151 mph. In 1966 a new type the *2+2* was made to carry four people. The maximum speed was dropped to 137 mph and the headlamp fairings were removed. In 1971 a new version was introduced powered by a V-12 engine. Above is pictured the 1966 model.

From speedster to GT coupé

Very few sports cars were made before 1914, but they became very popular in the 1920s. In America sports cars were called speedsters. European sports cars in the 1920s were either light two-seaters like the French *Amilcar* and the *Salmson* or larger four-seaters. Amongst these, the *Bentley, Sunbeam* and *Vauxhall* were very popular. The American speedsters used parts from ordinary cars built into special bodies.

In Europe in the 1930s cars like the *Wolseley Hornet* and the *M.G. Midget* were made, which were based on ordinary mass produced cars. A lot of these were sold but though they were fun to drive they were not the best of sports cars. The cars made by hand like the *Alfa-Romeo, Aston-Martin, Frazer Nash, Bugatti* and *Clement-Talbot* were much

better. They were also more expensive and not many of them were made.

By about 1955 sports cars became more streamlined. They were often developed from ordinary production models which were made to go fast. This was done by working on the engines to give them more speed and more power. They call this 'tuning'. *Renaults, Fiats* and *Fords* were all used by racing drivers, and the experience gained by racing cars made from standard saloons made it possible for the engineers to make better cars.

Open two-seaters were popular until about 1960, but now people want more comfort and they prefer the GT coupé type of sports car. Britain is the only country still making many open two-seater sports cars such as the *Sprite, Triumph TR6, Morgan* and *Jaguar.*

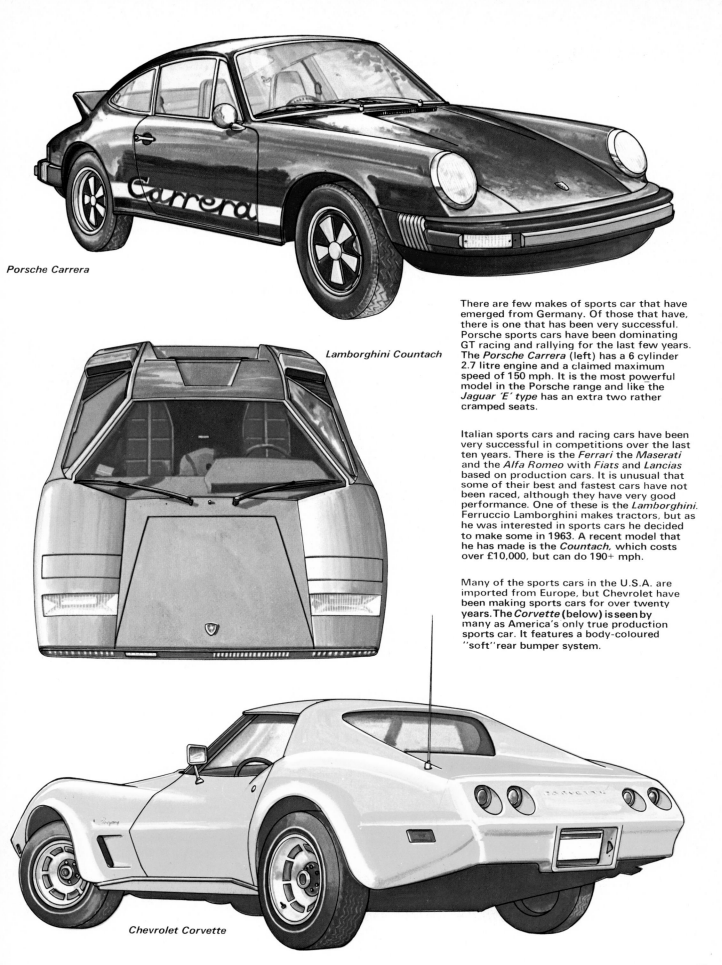

Porsche Carrera

Lamborghini Countach

There are few makes of sports car that have emerged from Germany. Of those that have, there is one that has been very successful. Porsche sports cars have been dominating GT racing and rallying for the last few years. The *Porsche Carrera* (left) has a 6 cylinder 2.7 litre engine and a claimed maximum speed of 150 mph. It is the most powerful model in the Porsche range and like the *Jaguar 'E' type* has an extra two rather cramped seats.

Italian sports cars and racing cars have been very successful in competitions over the last ten years. There is the *Ferrari* the *Maserati* and the *Alfa Romeo* with *Fiats* and *Lancias* based on production cars. It is unusual that some of their best and fastest cars have not been raced, although they have very good performance. One of these is the *Lamborghini*. Ferruccio Lamborghini makes tractors, but as he was interested in sports cars he decided to make some in 1963. A recent model that he has made is the *Countach*, which costs over £10,000, but can do 190+ mph.

Many of the sports cars in the U.S.A. are imported from Europe, but Chevrolet have been making sports cars for over twenty years. The *Corvette* (below) is seen by many as America's only true production sports car. It features a body-coloured "soft" rear bumper system.

Chevrolet Corvette

Launching a new car

(Picture 1)
A new car is first conceived by designers and stylists. They have to produce improved designs as well as incorporating the latest technical developments. They also are influenced by market researchers who advise them what sort of car the public will want. Since millions of pounds are involved, the final decision on whether or not to produce a new car is a very difficult one. The decision must be made by the main board of the company.

Drawingboard to showroom

Seeing a new car in a showroom it is easy to be unaware how much work and money is required to put it there. A new model is the result of months, and possibly years, of work for hundreds of people. Well before the first new model even comes off the production line millions of pounds will have been spent on making tools and changing the factory around. Parts of the factory may well have to be rebuilt and more machines may be needed.

The whole process starts when designers and stylists produce plans for a new car. Apart from a good design the new car must be easy to mass produce. Other people have the job of finding out exactly what sort of car people will want to buy. This is called market research.

Next a prototype of the new car is built and the design is tested. If the design is found to be good the factory will be prepared for production.

When a new car is put on the market, the manufacturers spend a lot of money on advertising. They also exhibit the car at motor shows attended by major car dealers from different countries.

1

(Pictures 2, 3)
Once the go-ahead is received on a new design a prototype is built at the factory. For each new model ten or more prototypes may be built costing more than £30,000 each.

2

3

(Pictures 4, 5)
The next stage involves testing the prototype. This is done in two separate ways—in the factory and on the road. In the factory they have special laboratories where every part of the new car is put through extreme tests. In these laboratories, specialists are working continually to make parts more dependable and safe. In this way they also contribute to the design of future cars.

4

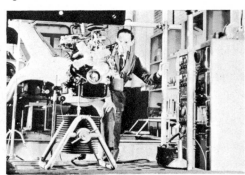

5

6

7

8

9

10

11

12

13

14

15

(Pictures 6, 7, 8)
The fully assembled prototype is then tested out on the road. The car is exposed to the conditions that might be found in the many parts of the world in which it will be sold. It is also a check on the results of the laboratory testing. It is at this stage that it is most difficult to keep the new car a secret, so on road tests the prototypes are often cleverly disguised. On the manufacturers own testing ground the car will be put through other tough tests. These include deliberately crashing into concrete barriers.

(Pictures 9, 10)
With the experimental stage successfully completed the process of making the new car begins. The factory is re-equipped, and its layout rearranged. Dies are cast and the components pressed.

(Picture 11)
With the assembly line set up, cars in the making move along the belts. Various parts of the car are assembled separately. With precision timing the various parts are finally brought together and the car comes off the assembly line completed.

(Pictures 12, 13)
After inspection and timing the completed car is tested under its own power. Ready to be sold it is sent out to showrooms throughout the world, by rail, road, and sea.

(Picture 14)
For the final stage the salesmen and public relations experts take over. Much money is usually spent on advertising a new car. Its first appearance is often at one of the International Motor Shows.

(Picture 15)
More publicity can be gained by entering the new car in a motor rally. From the buyer's point of view, this form of competition really tests the car. Many people who buy cars take this into account when choosing a new car.

Record breaking

There always have been men who like to drive their cars fast. In 1904 at a normal race meeting at Ostend in Belgium, for the first time a man travelled at faster than 100mph. Louis Emile Rigolly drove a 100hp *Gobron-Brillie* (right) at 103·56mph over a timed kilometre.

1904 Rigolly's Gobron-Brillie.

In 1922, Kenelm Lee Guinness pushed the world record to 133·57mph in his 350hp 12 cylinder, aero-engined, *Sunbeam* (right). This was the last time the record was broken at Brooklands.

1922 Guinness's Sunbeam

The last record to be made on a road was by Ernest Eldridge in his 1924 car, *Mephistopheles* (right). The 'Mad Englishman', as he was known, drove his reconstructed 1908 *Fiat* with its new engine at 146mph.

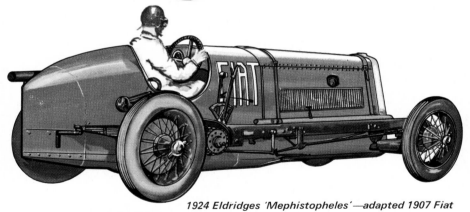

1924 Eldridges 'Mephistopheles'—adapted 1907 Fiat

From 1927 to 1935 all the records were broken at Daytona Beach in the US. The 200mph barrier was broken when Sir Henry Segrave drove his 1000hp *Sunbeam* (right) at 203·79mph in 1927.

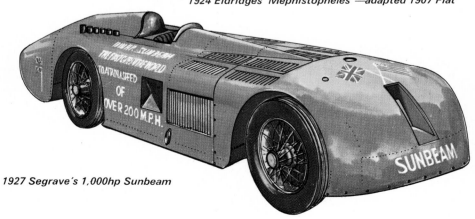

1927 Segrave's 1,000hp Sunbeam

1935 Sir Malcolm Campbell's 'Bluebird'

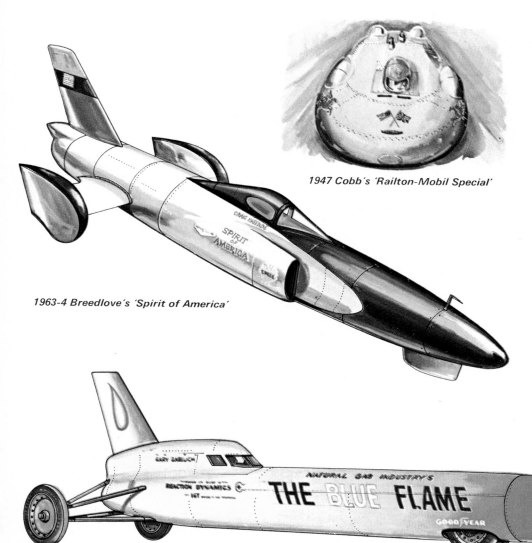

1947 Cobb's 'Railton-Mobil Special'

1963-4 Breedlove's 'Spirit of America'

1970 Gabelich's 'Blue Flame'

Nine years later the record was pushed over 300mph by Sir Malcolm Campbell in the special Rolls-Royce Campbell car, nicknamed the *Bluebird* (right). The new record was 301·13mph and the run was made at Bonneville Salt Flats, Utah, in the US. *Bluebird*'s engine was the forerunner of the Merlin aero engine to be used in the famous World War II warplane, the *Spitfire.*

It was not until after the War that a car was driven faster than 400mph. On the south-north run at Utah, John Cobb drove his *Railton-Mobil Special* (left) to 403·135mph. The official record, calculated from this and the north-south run was 394·20mph.

Again at Utah, in 1963 and 1964 the record was pushed beyond 400mph and then 500mph by Craig Breedlove in his jet powered *Spirit of America* (left). Controversy surrounded these records and others made by competitor, Art Arfons, in his jet car, *Green Monster.* Existing rules excluded vehicles not driven through the wheels. Breedlove's 526·28mph record of October 15, 1964 was finally recognized. Later Breedlove abandoned this car in favour of a four-wheeler *Spirit of America—Sonic I.* The best performance achieved in the second car was 613·995mph on November 15, 1965.

The record was broken in October 1970 on the Salt Flats by Gary Gabelich. He was driving a specially built 'car' called the *Blue Flame* (below left). It was built and sponsored by the United States Institute of Gas Technology. Liquified gas and hydrogen peroxide are used as propellants. The tyres were handmade, about three feet high, and inflated to 350 pounds per square inch. The *Blue Flame* covered the measured mile in two runs at speeds of 617 and 627mph setting a new record of 622·407mph.

Drag Racing

Drag racing is a form of sprinting in a straight line. Two cars, known as dragsters take part in each race. The cars have huge rear wheels and powerful engines. The fastest have tuned up V8 engines. They can cover the quarter mile in under 7 seconds. At the start they spin their wheels and disappear in clouds of smoke. By the time the quarter mile is completed they are travelling at over 200mph and parachutes are needed to stop them.

35

Blessing or disaster problems of the car era

The real problems of the motoring age are not caused by the car itself, but by the great numbers of them there are on the roads. The more cars there are, the more roads are required. The better the roads become the more people find the car convenient. So the numbers of cars and the cost of finding room for them seems to spiral upwards endlessly. In many cities where thousands of people go to work by car the situation is constantly on the brink of chaos. Huge time-wasting traffic jams are an everyday occurrence (right).

Japanese "Police Pollution Squads" check car exhausts in Tokyo's congested streets in an attempt to control air pollution (above).

Concentration of traffic, especially in cities, has many unpleasant side effects. The fumes given out by thousands of cars can poison the atmosphere and even cause a special type of fog known as smog. Apart from gases, car exhaust contains solid matter.

From horses to traffic jams

There are more than 217 million vehicles in the world. Most of them are in North America and Europe. In some countries the road system has not changed very much since the days of horses. In big cities there were traffic jams even in those days. Today there are many problems because people were too busy producing and buying cars to think about living with them. At first, when only the rich could afford cars, it was easy to make room for them. As ordinary people got higher wages so they could afford cars. They could then live further away from their work. As people got richer so more and more could buy cars.

Convenience at a price

With so many cars the roads were just not able to take the traffic. The answer was to build motorways, flyovers, under-passes, and by-passes. These, too, had their problems. In some countries there is not much land to spare. New roads eat up much land and cut fields and housing areas in half. A footbridge over a motorway can cost £30,000. Good houses have to be knocked down and others near the road lose their value. Great numbers of cars also make a lot of noise, dirt, and dangerous fumes.

The motor car is providing pleasure and convenience for millions of people. At the same time it is polluting the environment and menacing life.

Traffic can flow freely, but at great expense. This view (right) of Detroit's freeway system shows how greedy for land the solution can be. Note, how the road cuts the town in two.

Public versus private transport

In some capital cities, like Rome and New York, they have thought about banning cars altogether. Few people will accept this solution. They think they should be free to own a car if they want to.

Heavy taxes on cars and petrol is another way of reducing the number of cars. So are road tolls and parking meters. The trouble is that these are unfair on poorer people.

Better city planning is another answer. Roads can be built quite separately from pedestrian areas. Shopping precincts can be built completely free of traffic. Special roads are then taken to the backs of the shops for service vehicles. Multi-storey car parks provide storage space for cars off the road, but conveniently close to the shops and offices. Another solution, quite common in the United States, is to build huge shopping centres in the suburbs where there is plenty of space for car parks. Better use can be made of existing roads by stricter traffic control. This could include more one-way systems and computer-controlled traffic lights.

A car may carry only one person to work. A bus can carry fifty or more. Some people say the real answer lies in a cheap efficient public transport system. Existing systems are a combination of buses, underground and overground trains and even overhead monorails. So far these systems seem unable to cope with congestion.

An electric cabin network

Research is going on in several countries looking for an ideal city transport system. One idea involves small plastic cabins electrically driven over a computer controlled complex system of track. The track would be cheap and light so that it could go practically anywhere. Passengers would choose their destination on a map and receive a card. This card would then be fed into a slot beside the seat and the cabin would go automatically to the destination. This system has many advantages. They include relative cheapness, freedom from noise and pollution, higher average speed, and ability to handle heavy traffic.

This system, or ones similar to it, will probably provide a practical solution to congestion in the cities.

People must decide for themselves which is the more important. Freedom for everybody to travel the way they want or an efficient transport system.

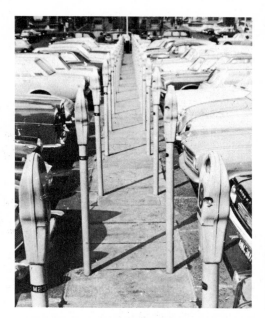

One method of rationing the space in crowded city centres has been parking meters (left).
If parking is expensive many motorists will be put off using their cars. Instead they will use public transport. In the future cars may be fitted with meters. These could measure the distance travelled and the time spent in crowded areas. Motorists could then pay for the amount they use the roads.

In the US., suburban shopping centres are built to serve cities where there are too many cars in the central area (below). In these centres people can buy most things they need. This saves making journeys to the city centre.

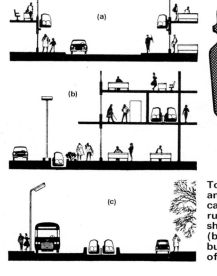

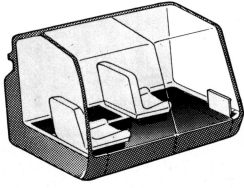

Tomorrow's answer to congestion, pollution, and noise in the cities could be this simple cabin (above). Cabin tracks are light and can run almost anywhere (left). Some possibilities shown are: (a) along the sides of buildings, (b) along the sides of roads and through buildings, (c) along the central reservation of a road.

Grand Prix racing

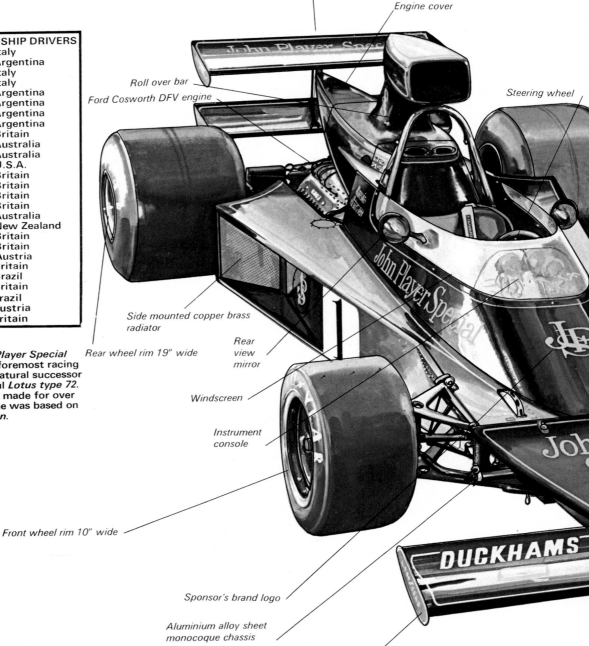

WORLD CHAMPIONSHIP DRIVERS	
1950 G. Farina	Italy
1951 J. M. Fangio	Argentina
1952 A. Ascari	Italy
1953 A. Ascari	Italy
1954 J. M. Fangio	Argentina
1955 J. M. Fangio	Argentina
1956 J. M. Fangio	Argentina
1957 J. M. Fangio	Argentina
1958 M. Hawthorn	Britain
1959 J. Brabham	Australia
1960 J. Brabham	Australia
1961 P. Hill	U.S.A.
1962 G. Hill	Britain
1963 J. Clark	Britain
1964 J. Surtees	Britain
1965 J. Clark	Britain
1966 J. Brabham	Australia
1967 D. Hulme	New Zealand
1968 G. Hill	Britain
1969 J. Stewart	Britain
1970 J. Rindt	Austria
1971 J. Stewart	Britain
1972 E. Fittipaldi	Brazil
1973 J. Stewart	Britain
1974 E. Fittipaldi	Brazil
1975 N. Lauda	Austria
1976 J. Hunt	Britain

The Formula I John Player Special (right) is one of the foremost racing cars today. It is the natural successor to the very successful *Lotus type 72*. Lotus cars have been made for over 26 years. The first one was based on the 1930 *Austin Seven*.

Adjustable rear aerofoil

Engine cover

Steering wheel

Roll over bar

Ford Cosworth DFV engine

Side mounted copper brass radiator

Rear view mirror

Rear wheel rim 19" wide

Windscreen

Instrument console

Front wheel rim 10" wide

Sponsor's brand logo

Aluminium alloy sheet monocoque chassis

Adjustable front spoiler

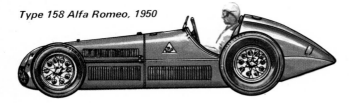

Type 158 Alfa Romeo, 1950

Alfa Romeo racing cars were very successful before the war. The Type 158 (above) was almost unbeatable until 1951, but the firm gave up racing in Formula I after that date. Fangio was a racing mechanic and started racing in 1948. He became World Champion at 40 and retired in 1958 at the age of 47.

Mercedes-Benz W196 1954

The *Mercedes-Benz* Grand Prix cars were most famous between 1934 and 1939. These giants, with 5.7-litre 8 cylinder engines went at more than 200mph. Mercedes started racing again in the 1950s and won the World Championship in 1954 and 1955 with the W196 (above).

Danger and expense

By nature, human beings like to win races. Chariots, horses and bicycles have all been used in competitions, but nothing has been so fast as motor racing. It is a dangerous sport, like many others, but an error of judgment on the race track can mean death or serious injury to any of the drivers involved. Racing drivers have to be very fit, skilled and experienced.

Rules are made for the production of all types of racing cars—these rules are international and are called the Formula. Formula I Grand Prix rules are changed about once every six years, and there is a limit on the size of engines which can be used. At present the limit is 3 litres or 1½ litres super-charged. Some have 8, and others 12, cylinders, and top speeds of over 200mph.

A Formula I car will cost over £35,000. Ford-Cosworth engines are about the only large manufacturers who are still directly involved with Grand Prix racing cars. Most of the other car firms have found Grand Prix racing to be too expensive for the credit or experience which can be gained. Oil and tyre firms still sponsor. Support is also given by various companies.

1975 John Player Team Lotus drivers

Ronnie Peterson (above) was born in Orebro, Sweden in 1944. He joined the team in 1973.

Jacky Ickx (above) was born in Brussels, Belgium in 1945. He joined the team in 1974.

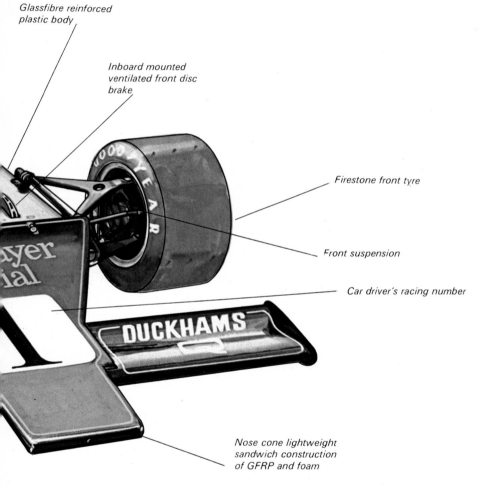

Glassfibre reinforced plastic body

Inboard mounted ventilated front disc brake

Firestone front tyre

Front suspension

Car driver's racing number

Nose cone lightweight sandwich construction of GFRP and foam

Vanwall 1957

The *Vanwall* (above) driven by Stirling Moss in the British Grand Prix in 1957 was the first British car to win a major Grand Prix since 1924. The first *Vanwall* Formula I racing car was made in 1954. They were the last successful front engine racing cars and were used until 1958.

Matra 1969

The French Matra company started to make racing cars in 1965. By 1968 they were making Formula I cars, and Jackie Stewart, the Scottish driver, raced for them. In 1969 he won the World Championship in a *Matra* using a Ford engine. Matra have now built a 12 cylinder engine of their own design which is one of the most powerful in use today.

The death toll and the safety revolution

Fatal Road Accidents		
Country		
W. Germany		
	1 in every 3,220 persons	
France	,, 3,460	,,
USA	,, 3,721	,,
Italy	,, 5,292	,,
Japan	,, 5,903	,,
UK	,, 7,404	,,

The table above brings out the big differences in the chances of being killed in a car accident in each of the big car countries. (Figures for 1972 except France 1969)

Menace on the roads

Each year 130,000 people are killed and possibly 1,700,000 are seriously injured. These startling figures refer not to a war but to road accidents in the western world. What is more, the numbers are rising rapidly.

For years cars have been made with little regard for the fact that they can kill and maim. Now that road accident figures have reached such proportions, people are at last beginning to realise that something must be done. Laws are being passed to ensure that cars are made safer, but progress is slow. Too many people still think it is more important that cars look good and go fast.

Life in their hands

Safety on the roads depends more on the driver than on the car itself. Many drivers do not have the necessary skill and rely on other road users for their safety. Others may suffer from physical disabilities such as poor eyesight. The reactions of many drivers are too slow, perhaps due to the effect of alcohol, or even old age. The solution to these problems depends not only on the car manufacturers, but on everybody who uses the roads.

The 'As safe as possible car'.

An artist's impression of a car incorporating features being researched, developed, or already in use. Cost prevents some of these being incorporated in the average family saloon for some years to come. More could be if only governments would pass laws to make them so. But not all experts agree on which features are really worthwhile.

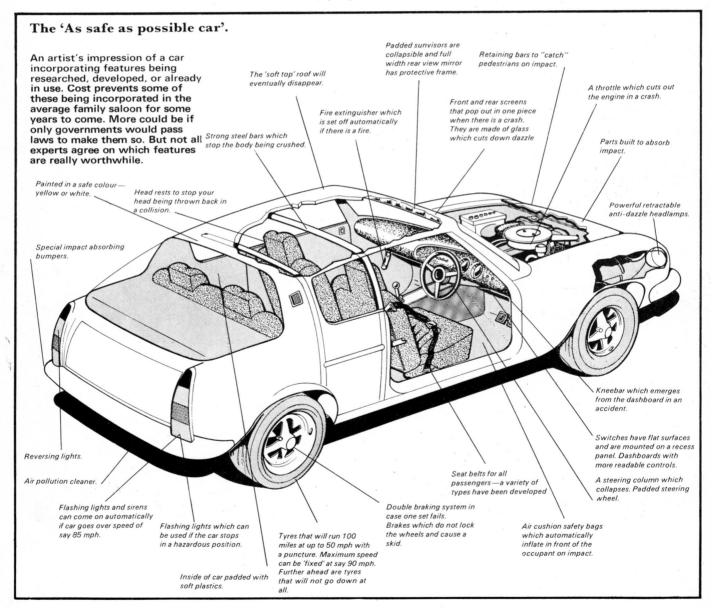

Padded sunvisors are collapsible and full width rear view mirror has protective frame.

Retaining bars to "catch" pedestrians on impact.

A throttle which cuts out the engine in a crash.

The 'soft top' roof will eventually disappear.

Fire extinguisher which is set off automatically if there is a fire.

Front and rear screens that pop out in one piece when there is a crash. They are made of glass which cuts down dazzle

Parts built to absorb impact.

Strong steel bars which stop the body being crushed.

Powerful retractable anti-dazzle headlamps.

Painted in a safe colour — yellow or white.

Head rests to stop your head being thrown back in a collision.

Special impact absorbing bumpers.

Kneebar which emerges from the dashboard in an accident.

Switches have flat surfaces and are mounted on a recess panel. Dashboards with more readable controls.

A steering column which collapses. Padded steering wheel.

Reversing lights.

Air pollution cleaner.

Flashing lights and sirens can come on automatically if car goes over speed of say 85 mph.

Flashing lights which can be used if the car stops in a hazardous position.

Tyres that will run 100 miles at up to 50 mph with a puncture. Maximum speed can be 'fixed' at say 90 mph. Further ahead are tyres that will not go down at all.

Inside of car padded with soft plastics.

Double braking system in case one set fails. Brakes which do not lock the wheels and cause a skid.

Seat belts for all passengers — a variety of types have been developed

Air cushion safety bags which automatically inflate in front of the occupant on impact.

Wankel's new engine

In the engines used in most cars the power from the explosion of the gas has to be converted into circular motion of the crankshaft. This very old idea works in the same way in a steam engine. The best way to increase the power given out by an engine, without making it bigger and heavier, is to increase the speed at which it rotates. This is about all that can be done with a piston engine, because there is a limit set by the movement of the pistons up and down the bores. The gas turbine is one way, but there is an even better engine which has a rotary piston and only a very small number of moving parts. This is called the Wankel engine and it may become the car engine of the future.

There were a lot of problems in the early stages. The gas escaped, and rubbing on the housing caused some parts to wear out too quickly, but in the end these were all put right. In the rotary piston engine, one revolution of the rotor is equal to three revolutions of the ordinary piston engine. One rotary piston can do the work of three pistons which travel up and down cylinders. The engine is quieter, gives less vibration and gives more power for its weight than the piston engine.

Audi NSU Ro 80

Above and below are two early production vehicles to incorporate the Wankel rotary engine. The relatively small German company NSU, backed Wankel and used his engine in the *Ro 80* (top). It has a 2 rotor 995cc engine and a maximum speed of 112mph.

Mazda RX-4

The Toyo Kogyo Group, Japan's third largest car manufacturer, hold the Wankel licence. They have several models in production and are reputed to be building Wankel engines at a faster rate than NSU. Above is the Mazda RX-4.

The Wankel Engine sequence

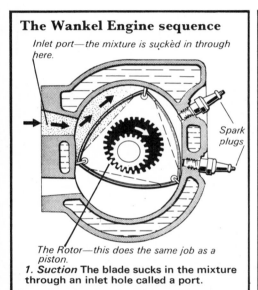

Inlet port—the mixture is sucked in through here.

The Rotor—this does the same job as a piston.

Spark plugs

1. Suction The blade sucks in the mixture through an inlet hole called a port.

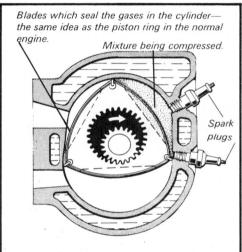
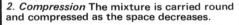

Blades which seal the gases in the cylinder—the same idea as the piston ring in the normal engine.

Mixture being compressed.

Spark plugs

2. Compression The mixture is carried round and compressed as the space decreases.

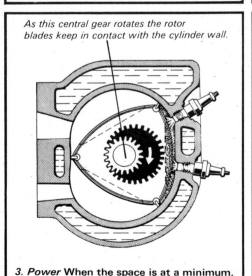

As this central gear rotates the rotor blades keep in contact with the cylinder wall.

3. Power When the space is at a minimum, the sparking plug ignites the mixture.

Exhaust port—the burnt gases are forced out through here.

4. Exhaust When the blade reaches the exhaust port, the burnt gas is swept out by the following blade. The cycle has already started again by this time.

Dr. Felix Wankel, a German engineer, had been studying the rotary piston engine for a long time. In 1951, with the German NSU car company, he made the first experimental engine. It took eight years before they were satisfied with the work, and the idea was patented all over the world.

Experimental cars for the future

Ford's experimental electric car
Several manufacturers have been experimenting with electric traction. The main problem has been the weight and size of the battery. Recent research has brought the possibility of a lighter and smaller battery which can be recharged at night by the house mains supply.

It is not easy to predict what is going to happen to car design in fifty years' time. Before then, all cars may well be fitted with automatic transmissions. Cars will be built to give the best possible safety and economy, and engines will not cause any pollution of the air. Design will be improved until there is almost no need for servicing after every 3 or 5,000 miles. Many components will be sealed after manufacture and will have fairly long lives. Some will be made of plastic.

When a certain number of miles have been travelled by the car, a light will come up on the dashboard telling the driver to change a part.

Much work has already been done producing practical alternatives to the petrol powered engine. Foremost in research have been gas turbines based on the jet engine used in aircraft, and electricity, already in use in milk floats. Atomic power, solar batteries, and even steam is being considered.

Many factors determine which of the many new inventions will be adopted for mass production. The important ones are that they should be economical on fuel, quiet, reasonably exhaust free, and light in weight. Above all they must be safe and cheap to mass produce.

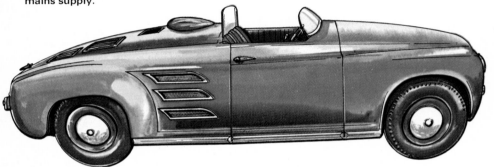

Rover gas turbine car

The main problem with gas turbines has been to produce a light enough engine that is also inexpensive.

This is the world's first gas-turbine motor car. It was designed and built by the British Rover Company. It could travel at nearly 152mph and went from 0 to 100mph in 13·2 seconds.

This is an American idea from General Motors for a city car. It is called the XP883. The body is made from fibre glass which will not rot. There are two motors. An electric motor driven by batteries at the back is used for moving off. When the car is moving the petrol motor at the front takes over. If extra speed is needed, both motors can work together.

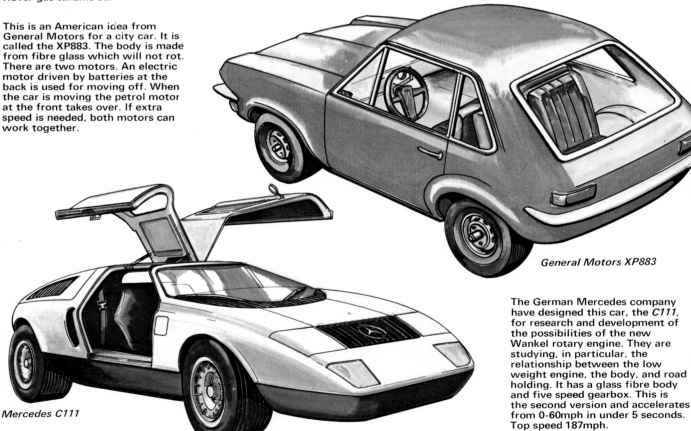

General Motors XP883

Mercedes C111

The German Mercedes company have designed this car, the *C111*, for research and development of the possibilities of the new Wankel rotary engine. They are studying, in particular, the relationship between the low weight engine, the body, and road holding. It has a glass fibre body and five speed gearbox. This is the second version and accelerates from 0-60mph in under 5 seconds. Top speed 187mph.

Projects supplement streamlining models

The shape of a car body governs the *wind resistance* produced when the car is driven fast. The more streamlined the shape, the less the wind resistance. Boxy shapes with vertical surfaces offer high wind resistance, and so reduce the speeds attainable. Smooth, curved shapes are much better, but are not always suitable shapes for cars. They do not leave enough room 'inside' for driver and passengers. One of the tricks in car body design, therefore, is to produce a good 'functional' shape with low wind resistance. You can learn more about this by experiment.

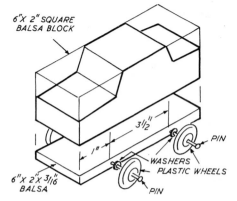

MAKING THE MODELS

The *chassis* is a 6″ × 2″ rectangle cut from $\frac{3}{16}$″ thick sheet balsa. Plastic wheels are mounted on pins in the positions shown. Use washers inside the wheels so that they rotate freely.

Body shapes (see below) are all carved from 6″ lengths of very light 2″ square balsa. To give a fair comparison, all bodies must weigh the same. Hollow out the bottom of each body so that plasticine can be added to bring each body to the same weight. Next, each body can be fitted in turn to the chassis, holding in place with pins pushed through from the bottom of the chassis.

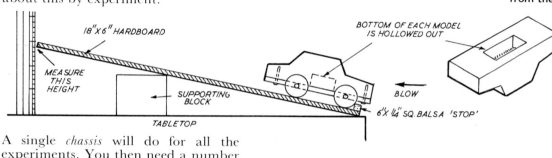

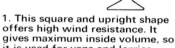

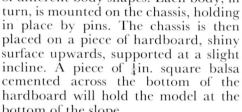

A single *chassis* will do for all the experiments. You then need a number of different body shapes. Each body, in turn, is mounted on the chassis, holding in place by pins. The chassis is then placed on a piece of hardboard, shiny surface upwards, supported at a slight incline. A piece of ¼in. square balsa cemented across the bottom of the hardboard will hold the model at the bottom of the slope.

The idea is now to blow hard against the model. This will produce a force acting on the model, due to wind resistance, tending to drive it up the slope. The model can be blown up. Simply move the supporting block backwards or forwards to adjust the slope until you have got a slope up which you can just blow the model. Measure the height of the slope with a ruler and make a note of it.

Now repeat the experiment with each of the other body shapes in turn. Each test should end up with a slightly different slope height, because the shapes are different. The height of the slope will be a measure of the drag coefficient. The greater the height the more wind resistance the shape must have had, to be blown up the steeper slope. For example, if for shape 1 there is a slope height of 2 inches, we can say that the drag coefficient is 2.

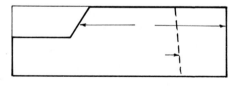

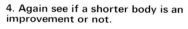

1. This square and upright shape offers high wind resistance. It gives maximum inside volume, so it is used for vans and lorries.

2. See if shortening the body reduces its wind resistance.

3. Same, but with the windscreen angled back. This should produce a little reduction in wind resistance.

4. Again see if a shorter body is an improvement or not.

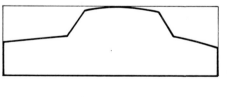

5. The majority of modern saloon car designs have a body shape similar to this. It is far less 'boxy', but streamlining can still be improved.

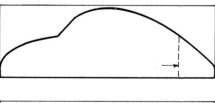

6. Streamlining is better but the curved outline is broken by a 'flat' where the windscreen appears.

7. See if cutting the body short makes any difference. You may find that this will *increase* the wind resistance.

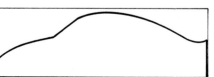

8. This is the popular 'fastback' tail end on a streamlined shape. In some cases it can decrease the wind resistance, and in others *increase* it! See how it works out on your model. If *too* streamlined, it can tend to lift off at high speeds, like an aeroplane!

How to be a car designer

Designing a car is rather like putting a jigsaw puzzle together. Engineers are responsible for the design of engines and gearboxes, transmissions, suspensions, and all the working parts. Someone then has to produce a car shape into which all these parts together with the driver and passengers can fit, in their proper positions. This is probably the most interesting part of car design, and these project pages show how you can design any type of car, starting with the basic components. We shall be working to a scale of 1/20th full size.

The basic 'engineering' parts required are an engine and gearbox, a radiator to match the engine size (unless the engine is air-cooled), wheels, and a back axle unit or differential.

Opposite are drawn outline shapes of all these components in various sizes, all to 1/20th scale. Trace these on to thick card or sheet balsa and cut out carefully.

Below are shown parts for making a scale model of a human figure, 5ft 10ins tall. The pivoted joints enable the figure to be set to any position. Cut out parts A, B, C, D, E, F and G very carefully in thick card or thin sheet balsa and use pins, passed through the pivot points, to assemble the model. Cut off the excess lengths of the pins and bend over to hold them in place.

The car designer has to try to cater for everyone, but the only way he can really do this is to work with a figure size which will be big enough to suit the majority of people. He can then provide adjustment of the seat position, and so on, so that the car will equally suit smaller, and if possible also taller, people. It can become difficult catering for people over six foot when designing a minimum size car!

You also need *data* or information on what are usual component and engine sizes for different types of cars. This information you can get from *specifications* of full size cars, such as you can find in books on cars, brochures given away by car manufacturers, or car magazines.

500 C.C. 750C.C. 1000-1500C.C.

ENGINES – WITH GEARBOXES

4-CYLINDER 6-CYLINDER
2-3 LITRE IN-LINE

V-4 V-6 V-8
V-4 – 2 LITRE
V-6 – 3 LITRE
V-8 – 4 LITRE
2-4 LITRE VEE

RADIATORS
500 – 750 1 LITRE 1·5 LITRE 2 LITRE 3 LITRE 4 LITRE 5-7 LITRE

5-7 LITRE
V-8

WHEELS – DOTTED OUTLINES SHOW ALTERNATIVE TYRE SIZES

15" 13" 11" 10"

ALL THESE PATTERNS ARE FULL SIZE FOR 1/20 SCALE

DIFFERENTIAL

WHEELBASE

Start a car design data book in which you record the following information on as many different cars as possible. Type (e.g. 4-seat saloon, 2-seat sports, etc), Engine size, Wheel size, Wheelbase dimension, Ground clearance.

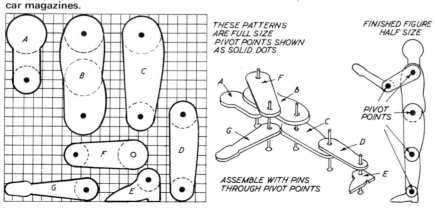

THESE PATTERNS ARE FULL SIZE
PIVOT POINTS SHOWN AS SOLID DOTS

FINISHED FIGURE HALF SIZE

PIVOT POINTS

ASSEMBLE WITH PINS THROUGH PIVOT POINTS

The wheelbase dimension is the distance between the centres of the front and rear wheels. It is one of the most important dimensions of all, for car design starts with this. You cannot afford to guess a figure. Follow what other car designers have done before. If you are starting to design a 4-seat saloon with a 1500 cc. engine, for example, look up in your data book the wheelbase dimensions of all the cars of this type. You will probably find that they are all very much the same.

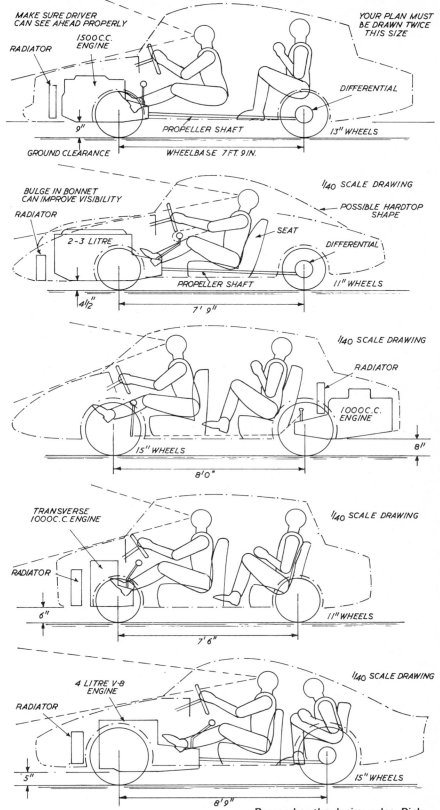

4-seat saloon with 1500 cc. engine

A suitable wheelbase dimension would be 7ft. 9ins. Draw vertical lines at $3\frac{7}{8}$ins. apart. Add suitable sized wheels (13 inches) using the pattern. Now use the 1500 cc. engine pattern to find a suitable engine position, giving a suitable ground clearance (say 9 inches). Draw round the engine and the radiator. Use the figure model to get a position where the driver can reach all the controls. Finally, fit in the rear seat passenger.

2-seat sports coupé

For improved performance we will use a 2–3 litre 6-cylinder engine, and reduce the wheel size to 11 inches to give really rapid acceleration. Checking with the data book will show that a 7ft. 9in. wheelbase dimension will be about right. Ground clearance reduced to $4\frac{1}{2}$ inches enabling us to set the bigger engine as low as possible. The driver will have a straight-arm, reclining driving position, and so the gear lever must be extended.

4-seat saloon with rear engine

This design could start with: 1000 cc. engine, 8ft. wheelbase dimension, 15 inch wheels, ground clearance 8 inches.

Placing the engine in the rear gives more body room, and also a flat floor since no propeller shaft is required. A short nose gives good driver visibility, but very little 'boot' space.

4-seat saloon, with front wheel drive

With a 1000 cc. engine, a 7ft 6in wheelbase would be about right, with 11 inch wheels and 6 inches ground clearance. We can mount the engine across the body, or sideways, and save on the bonnet length required. No propeller shaft is needed. Plenty of room inside, with quite a short overall length. Luggage space is small.

2+2 GT coupé

For this design a 4 litre V-8 engine is adopted. A suitable wheelbase would be 8ft 9in, with 15 inch wheels. Ground clearance can be as little as 5 inches. This will enable the large engine to be low slung, improving stability and permitting a 'dropping' bonnet line. Note in this layout that rear seat space becomes very cramped.

None of the five models shown should be *copied* as finished designs. They are merely planned to show *how* to design a car to a particular specification. In fact, each drawing incorporates one or more deliberate mistakes, or details which could be improved upon quite a lot. By working out your own designs in each case you should be able to finish up with better results.

Equally, of course, by writing your own specifications you can produce many other different designs.

Remember the design rules. Pick a suitable wheelbase dimension and suitable wheel size. Draw out to 1/20th scale. Next position the engine and gearbox, and the radiator and propellor shaft if needed. Use the figure model to position the driver and passenger properly seated. Sketch in the body shape.

Building and improving a car design

The car design so far is only a flat *side view* shape. To turn it into a three-dimensional shape, an end-on view drawing has to be prepared. The stability of the car, and how it responds to steering control, will be affected by the track or distance between the centre line of the wheels. The wider the track, in general, the safer and more stable the car will be. Too great a track, though, can be just as bad as not enough. The overall width is less important, but governs how much sideways room there is inside.

The final test of your car design is to turn it into a three-dimensional model. Car designers use models a lot, to check shapes.

Stage 1 Start by cutting out a rectangular piece of ¼" hard balsa sheet to the exact both length and width of your design, to 1/20th scale (working out a suitable width). Mark on the wheelbase position and cut notches, as shown, to take the wheels at their correct TRACK.

Stage 2 For the body block you will need a piece of balsa the same dimensions as the first sheet but equal in depth to the body height (not the overall height), less ¼" (to allow for the base piece thickness). You may find it easiest to use two balsa blocks, cemented together, rather than a single solid block. Pin the body block(s) to the base piece and mark on the side view shape.

Stage 3 Cut out arches in the body block to clear the wheels.

Stage 4 The body block can now be cemented to the base piece of 'pan' and carved to body shape.

Stage 5 Finish by rounding off to final shape.

Stage 6 The shaped body should now be sanded smooth and given several coats of sanding sealer, sanding between each coat. When you have got a really smooth finish all over, paint in a suitable colour with model aeroplane dopes.

If the paintwork appears blotchy, this is because you have not used enough sanding sealer. Wait for the coloured dope to dry quite hard and sand down again. Repeat, until you have produced a good glossy finish all over.

Stage 7 The windows—and perhaps the front of the bonnet—should then be painted with matt black. If your hand is a bit 'shaky' when using a paint brush you can make a neater job of the windows by cutting their shapes out in black paper and gluing them on.

Stage 8 Try to find some plastic 'scale' wheels of the right size. Failing that, use wooden wheels which you can sand down to the right size. Fit these in place with pins, pushed into the 'pan'. Finally add the various items of 'trim'. Headlamps can be large drawing pins, or large silvered upholstery tacks. Bumpers can be bent from aluminium wire, or carved from balsa and covered with silver paper

In your car design data book, take a note of the track of all the different kinds of cars you can.

It is also useful to make a note of seat widths, and overall widths. A seat needs to be at least 18 inches wide to be comfortable, and a 21 to 22 inch width is usually the figure designers aim to achieve. This applies regardless of the *size* of the car. People need the same width of seat in a small car as a large one. In wider cars seats can be set farther apart for more comfort.

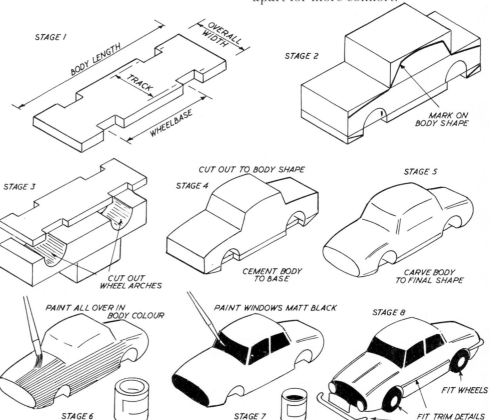

Improving on your car design

No car design is ever perfect right from the start. In producing a new full size car design perhaps a dozen or more different designs have to be drawn out, built up in model form, and finally discarded in favour of just one. The same thing can happen with your design. It may look much better as a drawing, than as a finished three-dimensional model. The answer here is to alter the shape of the model, as work proceeds, to correct what seem poor shapes.

This will usually show up at stage 4 (above). Having cut out the shape, although it is still 'square', it may not look quite right. If so, try altering the shape to see if you can improve it. If necessary, cut off the body block and start with another one. Remember, though, any altered shape must still give the same amount of 'inside room' as your plan shows.

Stage 5 (above) is another point where you can alter the body appearance by introducing curves, particularly on the bonnet lines. Designing an attractive bonnet and front end shape is probably the hardest part of all.

Study cars and photographs of cars to see how full size designers tackle these problems. Keep records and cuttings of what you consider 'good' and 'bad' designs. Develop your own ideas from the 'good' designs, and avoid the bad' ones'!

Index

Numbers in italics refer to illustrations

Entries in italics refer to names of cars

Accelerator pedal, 9
Accidents, 40
Advertising, 33
Air-cooled engine, 25
Alfa-Romeo, 19, 30, 31
Aluminium, 23
Amilcar, 30
Arfons, Art, 35
Ascari, A., 38
Asbestos, 8
Assembly, 21, 33
Aston-Martin, 30
Atomic power, 42
Audi NSU Ro 80, 41
Austin, 10
Austin, Herbert, 14, 22
Austin Seven, 14, *15*
Austin Ten 'Lichfield', 22
Austin-Healey Sprite, 30
Automatic transmission, 42
Auto-Union, 19
Axles, 3, 8

Ballot, 14
Battery, 9, 14
Battery driven car, 42
Bean, 14
'Beetle', 24, 25
Belgium, 34
Bentley, 19, 30
Benz, Karl, 4
Benz, first car, 5
Benz 1907, 10
Birmingham, 22
'Bluebird', 35
'Blue Flame', 35
Body, 9, 21
Body design, 43, 44, 46
Body shapes, 46
Bollée,
Bollée 1897, 5
Bonnet, 10, 11, 22, 23
Bonneville salt flats, 35
Bouton,
Brabham, Jack, 38
Brakes, 8
Brakes, drum, 8
Brakes, four-wheel, 14, 18
Brake pads, 8
Brakes, spoon, 8
Breedlove, Craig, 35
British Leyland, 22
British Motor Corporation, 22
B.M.C see British Motor Corporation
BMW 3.0Si, 26
Brooklands, 18, 34
Bugatti, Ettore, 18
Bugatti, 18, 30
Buick Electra 225, 29
Buick Motor Co., 28
Bulb horn, 10
Bulb horn, see also Motor horn
Bullnose Morris, 14
Bumpers, 23
By-passes, 36

Cadillac, V-16, 1930, 28
Cadillac Company, 28
Cadillac Fleetwood, 29
Campbell, Sir Malcolm, 35
Car design, 43, 44
Car parks, multi-storey, 37
Car shape, 43

Carburettor, 9
Car exports, 14, 26, 27
Car production, 10, 14, 26, 27
Car production, mass, 14
Carriage, Steam road, 3
Carriages, *3*
Cars in use, 36
Cars in use, New Jersey, 26
Chain drive, 7, *8*
Chariots, Roman, 3
Chassis, 3, 7, 9, *43*
Chauffeur, 10, 16
Chevrolet Camaro LT Coupe, 29
Chevrolet Corvette, 31
Chevrolet, 31
China, 3
Chrysler, 22
Chrysler Corporation, 22
Citroën 12, 23
Citroën GS, 27
Clark, Jim, 38
Coach-builders, 9
Cobb, John, 18, 35
Coil ignition, *9*
Coil spring, *8*
Compression stroke, *4*
Congestion, 36, 37
Connecting rod, 4
Crankshaft, 4, 41
Crossley, 30
Cylinder, 4

Daimler 1885, 5
Daimler engine, 4
Daimler, Gottlieb, 4
Dashboard, 10
Datsun Cherry, 26
Daytona Beach, 34
De Dion-Bouton 1898, 5
Design, body, 43
Design, cars, 43, 44
Designers, 32
Detroit, 22
Detroit freeway system, *36*
Dion, Compte de, 5, 6
Disc brakes, *8*
Distributor, 9
Dodge, 22
Dodge cars, 1914–1974, 23
Drag coefficient, 43
Drag racing, 35
Dragster, 35
Drum brakes, *8*
Dunlop, John Boyd, 6
Durant, William C., 28

Economy cars, 14, 15
Egyptians, 3
Eldridge, Ernest, 34
Electric cabin network, 37
Electric car, 42
Electric car, Ford, *42*
Electric lamps see Electric Lights
Electric lights, 11, 14
see also Headlamps
Electric spark, 9
Electric wiring, 21
Engine, air-cooled, 25
Engine, Ford-Cosworth, 38
Engine, gas, 4
Engine, gas turbine, 42
Engine, petrol, 4
Engine, rotary, 41
Engine, steam, 3, *3*, 42
Essex 1922, 15
Exhaust, 4
Exhaust pipes, 19
Exports, 14, 26, 27

Fangio, Juan Manuel, 38
Farina,
Ferrari, Anzo, 31
Fiat 1914, 11
Fiat 126, 27
Fiat, 30, 31
Fiat Mephistopheles, 34

Fibre glass bodies, 42
First World War, 14
Fittipaldi, E., 38
Flyovers, 36
Flywheel, 4, 5
Ford 1939, 22
Ford, 30
Ford-Cosworth engine, 30
Ford electric car, *42*
Ford, first car, 13
Ford Galaxie 500, 26
Ford, Henry, 10, 12, 13, 14, 24, 28
Ford, Henry, first workshop, 13
Ford, Model 'T', 12, 14, *24, 25*
Ford Motor Co., 26
Formula 1, 38
Formula 1, racing, 38
Four-stroke cycle, 4
Four-wheel brakes, 14, 18
Frazer Nash, 30
Front-wheel drive, 23, 45

Gabelich, Gary, 35
Gas engine, 4
Gas explosion, 4
Gas lamps, 11
see also Headlamps
Gas turbine, 42
Gearbox, 7, 44
Gearbox, five-speed, 42
Gears, 7
General Motors Corporation, 2, 6, 28, 29
General Motors XP883, 42
Glass fibre see Fibre glass
Gobron-Brillie, 34
Goggles, 10
Grand Prix France, 17
Grand Prix, United States, 38
Grand Prix, see racing
Green Monster, 35
Ground clearance, 45

Hawthorn, Mike, 38
Headwear, 11
Headlamps, 23
Hill, Graham, 38
Hill, Phil, 38
Hire purchase, 10
Hispano-Suiza, 14
Hitler, Adolf, 24
Holden, 29
Holden Monaro GTS, 29
Horses, 3, 16
Hulme, Denny, 38

Ickx, Jacky, 39
Ignition, *9*
Imports, 14, 26, 27
Imperial, 22
Independent suspension, 23
Inspection, 33
Institute of Gas Technology, United States, 35
International Motor Shows, 33
Isotta-Fraschini, 14

Jaguar 'E' Type, 30, 31
James' steam carriage, 3
Japan, Toyo Kogyo Group, 41
Jarrot, Charles, 7
Javelin, 31
Javelin SST, 31
John Player Special

KdF-Wagen, 25

Lancia Aprilia 1939, 23
Lancia Lambda F125, 15
Landaulet, Austin, 10–11
Lamborghini, Ferruccio, 31
Lamborghini Countach, 31
Leaf springs, 8
Leather belts, 8
Leather suspension, 8
Lee Guiness, Kenhelm, 34
Lenoir, Jean Joseph, 4

Levassor, Emile, 4, 6, 7
Lotus, 38
Lotus, Team Drivers, 39
Lotus Type 72, 38
Luggage space, 45

Machining, *20*
Marcus, 4
Marcus 1874, 5
Magneto, *9*
Mass-production, 12, 14, 20, 21, 28
Matra Co., 39
Matra 1969, 39
Mazda RX-4 Coupé, 41
Mephistopheles-Fiat, 34
Mercedes, 1903, 6
Mercedes, 1914, 11
Mercedes C111, 42
Mercedes-Benz, 30
Merlin aero engine, 35
M.G. Midget, 30
Michelin brothers, 6
Minicar, 27
Miura see Lamborghini Miura
Model 'T' Ford, 12, 14, *24, 25*
Morris, 22
Morris, Bullnose, 14
Morris, W. (Lord Nuffield), 14
Mors, 6
Motor cycle, 4
Motor horn, 10
Motorways, 36
Multi-storey car parks, 37
Multi-twist horn, 11
Museums, Munich, 5
Museums, Science Museum, London, 5

Napier-Railton, 18
New Jersey, 26
Nordhoff, Heinz, 24
NSU RO 80, 41
Nuvolari, Tazio, 19

Oakland Motor Co., 28
Oil lamps, 11
Olds, R.E., 28
Oldsmobile Cutlass Coupé, 29
Opel, 26, 29
Opel Commodore GS Coupé, 29
Ostend, 34
Otto, Nikolaus August, 4
Otto cycle, 4
Otto gas engine, 4

Pack horses see horses
Pads, 8
Panhard, Rene, 6
Panhard 1902, 7
Panhard et Levassor 1895, 4, 7
Parking meters, 37
Pedal, accelerator, 9
Peterson, Ronnie, 39
Petrol, 14
Petrol engine, 4
Petrol pump, 14
Petrol vapour, 9
Peugeot 1896, 7
Peugeot 1905, 10
Peugeot Quadrilette, 14
Pinto, Ford, 20
Piston, *4*, 9
Plastic, 42
Platinum tube, 9
Plymouth PJ 1935, 22
Pollution, 36
Pontiac Firebird, 29
Porsche, Ferdinand, *24*
Porsche Carrera, 31
Power stroke, 4
Pressing, *20*
Prices, 10
Production see also mass production
Production, France, 27
Production, Great Britain, 27

Production, Italy, 27
Production, Japan, 27
Production, United States, 26
Production, West Germany, 26
Propellor shaft, *8*
Prototypes, 32
Public transport, 37
Pulleys, 8
'Punch', 16, 17

Race, Paris—Bordeaux, 7
Race, Paris—Madrid, 6
Race, Paris—Rouen, 6
Race, Paris—Vienna, *6*
Races, Road, 6, 7
Races, track, 18
Racing *see also* Brooklands
Racing *see also* Drag racing
Racing, Grand Prix, 7, 38
Racing drivers, 38
Radiator, 15, 23
Railton-Mobil Special, 35
Railways, 3
Renault 1902, 6
Renault, Marcel, 6
Rigolly, Louis Emile, 34
Road accidents, 40
Road accidents, figures, 40
Road deaths, *40*
Roadholding, 8, 23
Roads, 3, 16
Roger, 4
Rolls-Royce *see also* Campbell,
    Sir Malcolm

Rolls-Royce coupé F127, 14
Roman chariot, 3
Rotary engine, 41, 42
Rover gas turbine car, *42*
Running boards, 10, 15, 23

Safety, 23, 40
Saloon bodies, 15
Salmson, 30
Schwimmkübel, 25
Science Museum, London, 4
Scuttle, 11
Seagrave, Sir Henry, 34
Seat width, 46
Sealed components, 42
Second World War, 24
Servicing, 42
Slides, 8
Silver Ghost, Rolls-Royce, 14
Sloan, Alfred, 28
Smog, 36
Solar batteries, 42
Spare wheel, 15, 22
Spark, 4
Sparking plug, 4, 9, 41
Speed limit, 3
Speed records, track, 18
Speed records, world, 34, 35
'Spirit of America', 35
'Spirit of America—Sonic 1', 35
Spitfire, 35
Spoon brakes, *8*
Sprite, 30
Springs, leaf, 8

Stage coaches, 3
Steam engines, 3, *3,* 42
Steam road carriage, 3
Steering column, 10
Steering tiller, 7
Stewart, Jackie, 38, 39
Stingray, 31
Stone rollers, 3
Streamlining, 43
Stylists, 32
Suction, 4
Sunbeam, 30, *34*
Surface vaporiser, *9*
Surtees, John, 38
Suspension, 3, *8,* 44

Testing, 21
Three-dimensional model, *46*
Throttle valve, 9
'Tin Lizzie', 12
Toyo Kogyo Group, Japan, 41
Track, *46*
Tracks, 3
Traffic jams, 36
Transmission, 8, 44
Transport, public, 37
Triumph TR6, 30
Tyres, iron, 6
Tyres, pneumatic, 5, *6,* 7, 10, 20
Tyres, solid rubber, 6, 16

Underpasses, 36
Unit construction, 9, 23

Valves, exhaust, *4*
Valves, inlet, *4*
Valves, opening and closing,
Vauxhall Magnum R300, 29
Vibration, 41
Volkswagen, 12, 24, *25,* 26
Volkawagen production, 24
Volkswagen prototype, *25*

Wankel, Felix, *41*
Wankel engine, 41, 42
Wankel engine sequence, *41*
Welded construction, 9
Welding, 20
Wheel, size, 44
Wheel, solid, 3
Wheel, spare, 15, 22
Wheel, spoked, 3
Wheel, wire, 11
Wheel, wooden, 3, 7, 15
Wheelbase *see* wheel, size
Wheeled carts, 3
Wind resistance, 43
Windscreen, 10, 21, 23
Wings, 11, 23
Wolfsburg, *24*
Wolseley, 22
Wolseley Hornet, 30
World speed record, 34, 35

Metric conversion table

1 in   = 25.4 mm
1 ft   = 0.3 m
1 mile = 1.6 km

1 sq ft = 0.09 sq m

1 lb   = 0.45 kg

Information and assistance were also given by:
'Motor' Magazine Library, British Leyland Motor Corp., Ford
Motor Co., General Motors, American Motors, Fiat Ltd.,
Volkswagen Ltd., Goodyear International Corp., Montagu
Motor Museum, Philip Batley, Dr. Alan Mayhew, Tim Nicholson,
Michael Twite (Sports Editor, 'Car'), David Burgess Wise
(Editor, 'Vintage').
Picture Acknowledgements:
PP. 16/17 Punch Publications Ltd., 21t Volkswagen Ltd.,
32/33 Fiat Ltd., 36t Keystone Press Agency Ltd., 36b Camera
Press Ltd., 37t Barnaby's Picture Library, 37m H. McLaughlin,
37b The Messerschmidt—Bölkow—Blohm Group.